Finding Aids to the Microfilmed Manuscript Collection of the Genealogical Society of Utah

DESCRIPTIVE INVENTORY OF THE ENGLISH COLLECTION

NUMBER 3

FINDING AIDS
TO THE MICROFILMED MANUSCRIPT COLLECTION
OF THE GENEALOGICAL SOCIETY OF UTAH

ROGER M. HAIGH, EDITOR

DESCRIPTIVE INVENTORY
OF
THE ENGLISH COLLECTION

BY

ARLENE H. EAKLE

ARVILLA OUTSEN

RICHARD S. TOMPSON

UNIVERSITY OF UTAH PRESS
SALT LAKE CITY
1979

The series Finding Aids to the Microfilmed Manuscript Collection of the Genealogical Society of Utah is funded in part by grants from the National Endowment for the Humanities and the University of Utah.

Number 1. Preliminary Survey of the Mexican Collection, 1978.

Number 2. Preliminary Survey of the German Collection, 1979.

10651-1
Gen

CONTENTS

Prepared with the assistance of the Center for Historical

Population Studies, University of Utah

Dean May, Acting Director

Anne Mette Haigh, Associate Editor

ACKNOWLEDGMENTS

We acknowledge the full and generous cooperation of the Genealogical Society of Utah. Our thanks are due George H. Fudge, Managing Director, for his early interest and continuing support. Raymond S. Wright, Acquisitions Department, has been a constant source of aid and advice. Paul Smart, Head, British Reference Section, has offered many helpful suggestions and much information. Frank Smith and David E. Gardner, whose work is well known to genealogists, are due a special note of thanks for their guidance and assistance.

The Institutional Funds Committee of the University of Utah provided the major financial support for this project.

A.H.E.

A.O.

R.S.T.

PREFACE

The largest collection of filmed manuscripts in the world, more than a million 100-foot rolls, is used only sparingly by the world's academic community and other genealogical researchers. This problem is a result of misinformation or lack of information about the Genealogical Society of Utah's collection. It is precisely this situation that the series Finding Aids to the Microfilmed Manuscript Collection of the Genealogical Society of Utah is designed to correct.

The scope of the collection is truly international. The declared intention of the Society is "to gather records on everyone who has ever lived." As astonishing as this statement may appear, this is the Society's goal. At the present time significant collections of microfilmed manuscripts exist for the United States, Europe, Latin America, and the Far East.

The bulk of this awesome collection is comprised of civil and parish registers of births, marriages, deaths, and whatever other kinds of information records of this type may contain. However, the remaining rolls of film alone constitute the largest collection of non-parish or non-civil register in the world! Included here is an amazing variety of types of materials--letters, maps, factory records, guild records, immigration material, to name a few. Whereas the parish and civil registers are usually adequately cataloged, these other kinds of records are not. The primary aim of the Finding Aids is to acquaint scholars with the nature and location of these historical manuscripts.

Three types of aids will be offered through the series: preliminary surveys, descriptive inventories, and bibliographic guides.

The preliminary survey is planned to give the researcher rather precise information about the holdings of parish and civil registers in large national collections. Designed as much to indicate regions within a national area where records are missing as those for which there are extensive holdings, the survey attempts to insure that those coming to use the collection are not disappointed, and that the library can have requested rolls available for the researcher upon arrival. The surveys also provide a general idea of the types of other materials that, for a variety of reasons, are a part of the Society's holdings in a given national area. Finally, the surveys identify sections for which existing cataloging is reliable and those for which it is not.

The descriptive inventory is a more precise bibliographic instrument. Aimed at collections less than 50 percent complete (as estimated by the Society), the inventories classify and record manuscripts and indicate film footage. The material is cross-referenced to give an interested researcher quite an accurate picture of holdings of particular types of records, holdings in given time periods, and holdings of various types of records within given geographic regions.

The bibliographic guide is the most detailed of the aids. It is designed to focus on smaller collections of previously uncataloged material. The bibliographic guide requires the reading of each roll of film in the collection and a precise description of its contents. The rolls are then cross-referenced by manuscript type, time span, region, etc. Bibliographic guides are planned only for collections the Society regards as complete.

The Finding Aids series represents the response of the University of Utah to needs expressed by the international community of scholars. This process began in 1976, when the University Institutional Funds Committee generously granted funds to the Department of History to bring in a team of social scientists to evaluate the scholarly potential of the collection and to make recommendations to facilitate its use. Jerome Clubb, Samuel Hays, and Jackson Turner Main represented researchers with an interest in holdings for the United States; and Louise Tilly, Lewis Hanke, and Richard Wall, the latter representing the Cambridge Population Studies program, investigated the potential of the international holdings. Their recommendations varied, but they were in complete agreement on two points: (1) The collection has fantastic potential for many types of scholarly research; and (2) a series of finding aids is urgently needed to make the collection more accessible to and more efficiently usable by scholars and other researchers.

As this book goes to press, preliminary surveys of the Mexican and German holdings have been published. These first three studies were made possible by additional funds specially allocated by the University of Utah and administered through the newly established Center for Historical Population Studies, Dean May, Acting Director.

Three more finding aids are in preparation, funded by a grant from the National Endowment for the Humanities: a bibliographic guide to a collection filmed in the Casa de Morelos, formerly the library of the Archdiocese of Michoacán, Mexico; a descriptive inventory of the filmed manuscript holdings for the state of New York; and a preliminary survey of the holdings for France.

These aids will be kept current through supplements issued as needed listing all pertinent, newly cataloged material. Supplements will be made available at cost to purchasers of the books.

If additional funding is available, the next three years will see the completion of a preliminary survey of Denmark; descriptive inventories of New England, Japan, and Louisiana-Georgia; and bibliographic guides for Scotland, Hungary, and Guatemala. Their publication will complete the series' first five years.

The series itself will then be reevaluated. The response of the academic community and researchers of all kinds, the needs of the Society, the availability of funds, and many other factors will be considered. If the results warrant continuation, another publication program will be outlined.

The authors and the publisher want these finding aids to be as effective a tool as possible. With this in mind, we earnestly solicit suggestions for improving their usefulness, which may be addressed to the series editor in care of the University of Utah Press.

Roger M. Haigh

INTRODUCTION

The Collection

The collection of English records has been a major element of the total program of acquisition for the Genealogical Society of Utah since its inception. Early and successful missionary work in the British Isles by the Latter-day Saints (LDS), the consequent heavy migration to Utah during the nineteenth century, and the absence of a language barrier, have encouraged extensive acquisitions from this geographic area. At the present time there are approximately 90,000 rolls of microfilmed materials in the Society's British collection, of which roughly 75,000 pertain to England.

Large scale retrieval of English records began in 1945; and the Society estimates that acquisition under present policies is now 50 percent complete. The principal types of material include:

Type	Percentage Completed
Census Records 1841-1871	100
Civil Registration Indexes	100
Probate Records -1857	95
Civil Probate Indexes	100
Parochial Church Records	40

The Genealogical Society's field operations in the British Isles currently employ four camera crews, but the rate of permissions to film has recently slowed operations to the point where only rarely are all cameras in full use. The general policy of the Society is to offer duplicate microfilm copies to archives and other repositories in exchange for permission to film. For Church of England records, permission to microfilm must sometimes be obtained from the diocesan bishop, the county archivists, and the parochial clergy--not always an easy requirement to meet. At various times the Society has filmed records in both the Public Record Office (P.R.O.) and in local archives, but the principal effort has obviously been devoted to records created and controlled by the Church of England.

The Inventory

The present Inventory is confined to unpublished material in the collection and is designed to indicate material available there, which may not be found in more than one other location. The principal aim is to provide the researcher with a broad summary of the collection and an indication of the variety of available material. Descriptive information has been kept to a minimum. The Inventory was prepared after a complete survey of the library's card catalog, and the original file cards from this survey have been deposited with the Center for Historical Population Studies at the University of Utah.

The Inventory is built upon the existing catalog system. The method of classification was constructed by condensing the library's 77 subject headings into a group of six which represent the basic nature of the generating sources and of the records themselves. At the same time, these six classes reasonably approximate standard archival classifications which scholars and others may encounter elsewhere: Government Records, Legal Records, Church Records, Corporation Records, Personal Records, and Research Aids.

The main part of this Inventory consists of sections covering the six classifications. Special procedures or features of each class are included in the prelude to each section. In general, the classifications are simple. "Government Records" include documents produced by officials other than clergy or courts of law. The records of the national government were filmed primarily in the Public Record Office, London; and the P.R.O. class numbers are given in each instance when available (e.g. Adm.=Admiralty, B.T.=Board of Trade, etc.). County government records comprise a limited class of militia records and scattered tax lists. The latter were, in fact, kept as records in the county archives but were created by authority of Parliament. Local government records are the major subdivision of this class.

Legal records are also divided into national, county, and local categories. The major national records acquired are the calendars of Chancery papers in the P.R.O. Some similar documents from Common Pleas and Exchequer are also available, but principal criminal court records and indexes are not. At the county level, papers of Commissions of the Peace--usually Quarter Sessions records--predominate. Local court records feature the manorial and borough courts; the holdings include a wide assortment of legal documents, including apprenticeship indentures, bastardy orders, and deeds.

The major source of church records is the Church of England; and within its records, marriage and probate information represents the largest element. The Inventory presents this material after the pattern of the Church's own diocesan organization. Nonconformist records and papers of the LDS mission are also noted.

Corporation records comprise a small but distinct category. They are mainly the papers of chartered companies, the largest group being from the city of Newcastle. As a general rule, these records have not received a high priority in the Society's acquisition program, and their coverage is therefore only occasional.

Personal records include documents generated by or about an individual or a family. Some eccentric deposits are included here, especially those which come under the heading of "collections." A number of researchers have compiled massive amounts of genealogical and other information, and the Society has filmed several of these extensive collections.

The section on research aids lists unpublished works which were created to assist investigations in the Society's British Collection. These aids are distinct from integral indexes or separate calendars which were published to augment a particular record.

Finally, the listing of the records of London--the most extensive for any single area--is presented in a separate section which follows the general system of classification: Government Records, Legal Records, Church Records, Corporation Records, Personal Records, and Research Aids.

A variety of tabular forms have been utilized in this Inventory, as a simple listing method proved inadequate. Parish registers, for example, are compiled regularly by the Society, thus the Inventory offers a frequency-distribution chart for those documents. Different and more elaborate forms of tabulation were also employed to cover the great variety and complexity of jurisdictions and records within the limits of the city of London. In each case where a special form of tabulation has been used, it is introduced in the prelude to the particular section.

The basic Inventory entry contains provenance, title, inclusive dates and number of rolls of microfilm. Provenance has been carefully identified, and in some cases modifications have been made to card catalog entries, especially where jurisdictions have changed. Thus, in view of the merger of various revenue departments and their functional reform, revenue papers have been classed under a loose heading of "exchequer," or they have been dispersed in county or local collections where they have been preserved. Wherever possible, titles are taken from the original. Dates shown are inclusive, and no attempt has been made to specify gaps. In most instances, catalog entries give specific dates, while some only note "missing years." The number of rolls refers to 100-foot rolls of 35mm microfilm. If the entry is given as "1" it means the record noted covers the entire film, even though it may be less than 100 feet. If the entry is given as "1 it." (1 item), the record noted is merely one of several included on that particular roll of film.

I GOVERNMENT RECORDS

The inventory of material considered government records includes those documents produced by officials other than clergy or courts of law. The national government records were filmed primarily in the P.R.O. in London. County government records comprise scattered tax lists and a limited class of military records which were kept in the county archives but were created by authority of Parliament. The inventory listing for these two groups follows a regular pattern.

The principal units of local government in England were, until the twentieth century, the manor, the parish, the town, and the borough. The documents produced in and by them are not precisely separable according to our scheme of classification, nor any other, primarily because of numerous political and judicial reforms which began during the nineteenth century. In addition the objectives of the Genealogical Society's acquisition program lend a particular emphasis to the collection. Therefore, the most efficient accounting is one which first recognizes the preeminence of vital records in the collection. After those, additional records of an administrative nature (accounts, vestry records, and poor law documents) have been noted. A third category comprises the remainder of miscellaneous local records and is contained in the main listing within this section of the Inventory. The extensive materials filmed for London are contained in the section devoted to that city. Local records will also be found under other section headings, especially "Church Records," which encompass marriage and probate documents, and "Legal Records," which include all local court records and various legal instruments such as deeds, bonds, and indentures.

Prior to the establishment of civil registration on a national basis in 1836, the parish register was the chief repository for vital information: births, christenings, marriages, and deaths. The parish register was transcribed annually

for the diocesan bishop. Both registers and transcripts constitute valuable
genealogical sources. The Genealogical Society has devoted the bulk of its
acquisition program to this type of record and to research aids which make them
accessible for genealogical work. One such project is the annual Parish and
Vital Records List, which presents, by parish or place, the identity and state
of processing of parish registers in the Society's holdings. While only those
items which have been processed internally by the Society are included, the List
is still comprehensive enough to preclude a parallel effort in this inventory.

The following table does, however, present a tabulation of the frequency
distribution of parish registers and bishops' transcripts. The number listed
under every half-century period represents the number of parishes for which the
Society holds any documents during that period of time. The documents might have
any or all types of vital information, and no attempt has been made to indicate
the precise number of years covered by each document--nor can this always be
detected from Frank Smith and David Gardner, Genealogical Research in England and
Wales, Volume II, Chapter 9. The percentages shown under PR (parish registers)
and BT (bishops' transcripts) represent the Society's estimates of the percentage
of pre-1813 documents which had been microfilmed by August, 1977. These percentages offer a rough guide to the completeness of coverage of all types of
vital information for each county.

The following list shows abbreviations of county names:

Beds.	Bedfordshire	Leics.	Leicestershire
Berks.	Berkshire	Lincs.	Lincolnshire
Bucks.	Buckinghamshire	Norf.	Norfolk
Camb.	Cambridgeshire	Nortn.	Northamptonshire
Ches.	Cheshire	Norld.	Northumberland
Corn.	Cornwall	Notts.	Nottinghamshire
Cumb.	Cumberland	Oxon.	Oxfordshire
Derby	Derbyshire	Rutl.	Rutland
Devon	Devonshire	Shrop.	Shropshire
Dorset	Dorsetshire	Somt.	Somerset
Durham	Durham	Staff.	Staffordshire
Essex	Essex	Suff.	Suffolk
Glos.	Gloucestershire	Surr.	Surrey
Hamp.	Hampshire	Sussex	Sussex
Heref.	Hereford	Warw.	Warwickshire
Herts.	Hertfordshire	West.	Westmorland
Hunt.	Huntingdonshire	Wilts.	Wiltshire
Kent	Kent	Worcs.	Worcestershire
Lanc.	Lancashire	Yorks.	Yorkshire

Parochial Registers

COUNTY	Total No. of Par.	-1500	1550-1599	1600-1649	1650-1699	1700-1749	1750-1799	1800-1849	1850-1899	1900-	PR %	BT %
Beds.	127	14	74	108	112	113	115	116	37	12	75	60
Berks.	162	17	62	73	99	112	119	119	47	21	71	0
Bucks.	206	6	32	44	57	66	72	77	58	27	40	0
Camb.	171	2	18	21	26	25	24	16	4	3	10	0
Ches.	130	1	6	6	11	11	15	14	4	3	?	?
Corn.	204	25	103	132	223	227	217	169	122	106	80	40
Cumb.	143	0	6	13	116	132	146	156	164	36	20	100
Derby	184	2	12	16	145	147	146	178	165	3	10	90
Devon	472	41	137	227	255	263	251	243	41	2	80	0
Dorset	260	2	4	3	5	3	4	4	1	0	8	0
Durham	93	3	27	41	49	51	59	48	14	11	85	0
Essex	405	14	70	102	100	109	103	97	12	7	60	0
Glos.	347	22	171	255	270	270	270	265	197	46	80	100
Hamp.	307	6	20	28	28	41	44	43	22	0	10	0
Heref.	223	3	11	17	32	36	30	27	19	4	15	100
Herts.	132	0	22	93	91	92	90	83	42	3	85	100
Hunt.	93	0	2	3	3	3	5	5	0	0	3	0
Kent	400	3	9	8	20	20	27	28	5	2	11	30
Lanc.	211	1	2	18	44	86	124	131	80	38	50	0
Leics.	256	4	238	278	272	272	273	286	223	23	80	100
Lincs.	627	3	664	684	691	693	695	703	761	71	85	100
Norf.	691	24	83	95	106	118	105	98	37	0	5	0
Nortn.	292	2	11	14	12	14	15	18	3	0	5	0
Norld.	96	0	5	18	80	93	106	106	35	0	85	0
Notts.	220	6	16	75	80	97	152	217	63	4	25	100
Oxon.	217	10	59	75	116	148	145	155	64	3	40	20
Rutl.	50	0	3	7	9	9	9	9	0	0	2	0
Shrop.	229	17	108	138	180	200	203	224	80	3	90	95
Somt.	486	1	48	79	65	49	45	43	1	0	3	0
Staff.	183	7	41	50	103	104	115	184	135	1	40	90
Suff.	504	61	135	146	160	172	160	152	109	19	35	100
Surr.	146	16	46	62	85	87	92	134	70	0	10	100
Sussex	305	15	83	101	108	111	106	99	66	5	40	0
Warw.	208	17	47	83	102	144	168	231	196	7	60	90
West.	68	2	10	14	38	40	43	69	64	2	10	100
Wilts.	318	3	18	30	45	55	58	59	42	17	25	0
Worcs.	209	42	69	140	157	173	137	155	129	57	90	100
Yorks.	751	28	175	404	436	483	516	566	212	8	20	10

Total percentage completed: PR   42.3%
BT   49.0%

Many Nonconformist chapels and some secular agencies kept vital records prior to the establishment of central registration. Once that process was begun, a commission of inquiry looked into the matter of nonparochial registers, and on its recommendation an Act was passed in 1840 which directed the General Register Office to receive about 8,500 such registers which had been identified by the commissioners. Additional registers were turned in to the Office after another commission was appointed in 1857. Still others remain outside the collection which is now located in the P.R.O. under classes R.G. 4-8. The Society has attempted to copy as many of these registers as possible. The next table follows the same format as that used for parochial registers, except that Society-coverage percentages are not available; and instead of parishes, other places of worship are counted. The count shows a concentration of these documents for the years between 1750 and 1849. Indeed, the vast majority fall between the years 1780 and 1830. Places of worship listed in the table correspond to those given for the year 1829 in volume one of the Parliamentary Gazeteer (Glasgow: 1840).

Nonparochial Registers

COUNTY	No. of Places of Worship	-1550	1550-1599	1600-1649	1650-1699	1700-1749	1750-1799	1800-1849	1850-1899	1900-
Beds.	71	0	0	0	0	0	1	1	0	0
Berks.	81	0	1	4	5	7	18	25	2	2
Bucks.	121	0	0	2	7	7	20	30	0	0
Camb.	85	0	1	3	9	9	19	29	4	1
Ches.	153	0	0	2	8	13	33	68	12	8
Corn.	320	0	0	11	14	16	19	49	2	1
Cumb.	105	0	0	8	24	28	34	36	8	0
Derby	182	0	0	2	2	4	22	39	2	0
Devon	217	0	0	2	11	21	43	82	4	1
Dorset	88	0	0	0	1	7	25	30	4	1
Durham	177	0	0	7	14	16	32	45	11	10
Essex	175	0	1	5	9	14	41	68	5	1
Glos.	177	0	1	10	23	25	43	66	1	0
Hamp.	128	0	1	5	15	22	35	43	53	1
Heref.	49	0	0	3	4	8	15	21	0	0
Herts.	62	0	0	3	7	8	18	33	1	0
Hunt.	36	0	0	4	7	7	9	12	6	0
Kent	210	0	1	7	14	17	34	59	0	0
Lanc.	504	0	0	4	15	26	148	250	27	15
Leics.	144	0	0	4	4	8	26	45	7	6
Lincs.	304	0	0	3	4	6	14	27	5	4
Norf.	181	0	0	1	12	16	39	112	9	6
Nortn.	153	0	0	2	4	9	31	59	1	1
Norld.	136	0	0	1	3	7	34	50	12	3
Notts.	152	0	0	3	5	7	9	45	4	4
Oxon.	99	0	0	2	3	3	4	8	16	3
Rutl.	13	0	0	2	2	2	2	1	0	0
Shrop.	102	0	0	0	4	4	4	31	0	1
Somt.	234	0	0	1	6	13	43	77	4	3
Staff.	213	0	0	1	2	4	25	66	0	2
Suff.	132	0	0	1	5	25	35	58	4	0
Surr.	101	0	0	4	5	4	12	25	2	1
Sussex	87	0	0	4	5	4	20	41	2	4
Warw.	108	0	3	6	9	10	37	55	11	7
West.	41	0	0	4	6	7	9	10	1	1
Wilts.	129	0	0	4	11	14	36	60	4	2
Worcs.	104	0	0	3	7	13	22	31	0	0
Yorks.	1,019	0	0	29	58	82	179	306	33	41

Another class of material, which the Society's catalog handles variously as civil records and church records, relates to the functions of government within the local setting and consists mainly of the varied materials generated by the parish vestry and its officers. The broad types of materials included are minutes and records of the parish vestry; accounts of church wardens, surveyors, and other officials; and papers and accounts of the "overseers of the poor" in their function as administrators of the Poor Laws. The materials which relate to local courts or their documents have been included in the section on Legal Records.

Following the same format as the previous listing, the next table counts the parishes for which some civil administrative records are available within each half-century time span. For additional miscellaneous local government records, see page 17.

Parochial Civil Records

COUNTY	Total No. of Par.	-1550	1550-1599	1600-1649	1650-1699	1700-1749	1750-1799	1800-1849	1850-1899	1900-
Beds.	127	0	0	1	6	18	15	16	1	0
Berks.	162	4	9	31	70	101	112	119	80	11
Bucks.	206	0	1	2	2	2	2	4	2	1
Camb.	171	0	0	2	2	4	5	7	5	0
Ches.	130	0	0	0	0	0	3	3	0	0
Corn.	204	1	2	6	17	25	37	41	30	21
Cumb.	143	0	0	0	1	5	5	10	9	3
Derby	184	0	1	1	1	1	1	1	1	1
Devon	472	2	6	6	8	8	8	9	3	0
Dorset	260	0	0	0	0	1	1	2	1	0
Durham	90	0	1	2	4	5	10	7	4	1
Essex	405	0	2	2	2	1	1	1	0	0
Glos.	347	0	2	2	2	2	3	3	3	0
Hamp.	307	0	0	0	0	1	1	2	2	2
Heref.	223	2	2	4	4	4	4	4	0	0
Herts.	132	3	12	24	50	83	104	116	84	10
Hunt.	93	0	0	0	0	0	0	0	0	0
Kent	400	0	0	0	0	0	0	0	0	0
Lanc.	211	1	1	1	4	13	19	22	13	10
Leics.	256	0	0	0	0	0	0	0	0	0
Lincs.	627	1	1	2	2	2	2	2	2	2
Norf.	691	0	1	1	2	3	3	3	1	0
Nortn.	292	0	0	0	1	1	1	1	1	0
Norld.	96	1	2	2	7	11	31	38	30	6
Notts.	220	0	3	12	36	77	93	112	84	27
Oxon.	217	0	0	4	4	4	4	11	9	5
Rutl.	50	0	0	0	0	0	0	0	0	0
Shrop.	229	0	0	0	0	0	0	0	0	0
Somt.	486	0	0	0	0	1	0	0	0	0
Staff.	183	0	0	0	0	0	0	0	0	0
Suff.	504	0	1	1	1	1	1	1	1	1
Surr.	146	0	0	0	1	3	3	3	0	0
Sussex	305	0	1	1	1	2	2	2	2	0
Warw.	208	13	21	40	83	158	194	221	195	47
West.	68	0	0	0	0	0	0	1	1	1
Wilts.	318	0	0	0	0	0	0	0	0	0
Worcs.	209	18	37	56	94	113	145	172	164	130
Yorks.	751	0	0	0	1	2	1	1	0	0

GOVERNMENT RECORDS: National

	Dates Covered	No. of Rolls
ADMIRALTY		
Papers		
Continuous Service Engagement Books, Indexed, Adm. 139	1853-1896	923
Indexes		
Index to Commission and Warrant Books, Adm. 6	1695-1742	2
Guide to Ships' Musters, Adm. 39	1667-1798	1 it.
Hired Armed Vessels, Adm. 41	1794-1815	1 it.
Coastguard and Revenue Cruisers, Adm. 119	1824-1857	1 it.
Index to Bounty Papers of the Admiralty Board, Adm. 106	1675-1822	1 it.
BOARD OF TRADE		
Papers		
Agreements and Crew Lists of Merchant Vessels, Indexed, B.T. 98	1835-1860	1748
Indexes		
Statistical Department, Passenger Lists[1]		1
Inwards, B.T. 26	1878-1960	
Outwards, B.T. 27	1890-1960	
Registers Received, B.T. 32	1906-1951	
Registers		
Register of Call Numbers for Agreements and Crew Lists, 1 vol.	1857-1860	

---

[1]The indexes to these classes were printed for the years prior to 1918 in Lists and Indexes, Supplementary Series, Vol. XI.

	Dates Covered	No. of Rolls
CENSUS OFFICE		
Papers		
Enumerators' Schedules	1841	924
	1851	1421
	1861	747[2]
	1871	2420
Registers		
Index of Place Names showing the Library Call Numbers for the 1841–1871 Census Records of England, Wales, Channel Islands and the Isle of Man, 7 vol.		
EXCHEQUER		
Papers		
Commissioners of Stamp Duties, Apprenticeship Books.		
Town Registers	1711–1811	34
Country Registers	1710–1808	
Lay Subsidies, Certificates of Residence, Indexed, E. 115	1547–1685	2 it.
Indexes		
Calendar of Clerical Subsidies, E. 179	1269–1663	1 it.
Guide to the Records of the Exchequer and Audit Office, Class List A.O. 3–24	1539–1910	1
Lay Subsidies, E. 359	1275–1377	1 it.
REGISTRAR-GENERAL		
Indexes		
General Registry		
Index to Civil Registration of Births, Marriages and Deaths for England and Wales	1837–1906[3]	1077

---

[2] On 16 mm film.

[3] The Society has the index only. Certificates of birth, marriage, and death must be ordered individually from Somerset House. Ordering information and costs can be determined by consulting the British Reference Area personnel in the Genealogical Society's library.

	Dates Covered	No. of Rolls
Principal Probate Registry		
Minor Courts, Distribution of Original Wills, Administrations and other Probate Records at Somerset House		1 it.
Calendar of Grants of Probate and Letters of Administration	1858-1957	542
Registers		
Register of Call Numbers to the Index of Civil Registration, 1 vol.	1837-1906	
Register of Call Numbers of the Grants of Probate	1858-1957	1 it.
TREASURY		
Papers		
Emigrants from England to North America, T. 47	1773-1776	1
WAR OFFICE		
Papers		
Regimental Description and Succession Books, W.O. 25	1756-1900	202
Certificates of Birth, Baptism, Marriage and Death (including wills and admins.), W.O. 42	1755-1908	156
Depot Description Books, W.O. 67	1768-1908	9
Soldiers' Service Documents, W.O. 97	1760-1900	1256
Cape Mounted Rifles	1830-1880	10
Horse Guards	1760-1800	1
Madras Artillery	1830-1850	1
Royal Artillery	1760-1854	125
Royal Regiment Artillery	1830-1860	3
Royal Canadian Regiment of Rifles	1840-1860	14
Royal Hospital Chelsea, Out-Pensioners	1761-1830	3
Royal Irish Invalids	1700-1810	5
Royal Newfoundland Companies	1800-1840	3
Various Regiments	1760-1900	1
Artillery Records		
Description Books, Records of Service, and Registers of Royal Artillery and Royal Horse Artillery, W.O. 69	1795-1906	107
Registers of Out-Pensioners, Kilmainham, Ireland, Army and Militia, W.O. 118	1759-1863	13
Regimental Registers of Pensioners, Chelsea Hospital, W.O. 120	1717-1857	31

Registers

    Register of Call Numbers for Army Records, 1 vol.

GOVERNMENT RECORDS: County

	Dates Covered	No. of Rolls
Papers		
Berkshire		
Militia Book	1796–1793	1
Protestation Returns	1641–1642	3 it.
Buckinghamshire		
Protestation Returns	1641–1642	1 it.
Land Tax Assessments[4]	1780–1830	23
Militia Papers	1790–1830	4
Poll Books	1722–1857	4
Register of the Names and Occupations of all Persons . . . between the Ages of 15 and 60 Years	1798	1
Register of Electors	1832–1841	5
Cambridgeshire		
Protestation Returns	1641–1642	1 it.
Cheshire		
Protestation Returns	1641–1642	1 it.
Land Tax Assessments	1780–1819	25
Register of Wills Proved in the District Registry	1882	1
Register of Gamekeepers	1771–1949	1
Hair Powder Tax Certificates	1797	1
Cornwall		
Protestation Returns	1641–1642	1 it.

---

[4]Cataloged by hundred. Land taxes are sometimes cataloged on a county basis, sometimes on a local basis.

	Dates Covered	No. of Rolls
Cumberland		
Protestation Returns	1641–1642	1 it.
Militia Lists	1797–1831	19
Devonshire		
Protestation Returns	1641–1642	1 it.
Dorsetshire		
Protestation Returns	1641–1642	1 it.
Durham		
Land Tax Assessments	1759–1831	16
List of Freeholders	1601–1609	1 it.
Poll Books	1675–1680, 1722	1
Essex		
Protestation Returns	1641–1642	1 it.
Freeholders' Books	1734–1815	1
Militia Returns	1809–1813	1 it.
Removal Orders and Settlement Papers	1651–1874	40
Ship Subsidy Money	1636	1
Hampshire		
Protestation Returns	1641–1642	1 it.
Hertfordshire		
Protestation Returns	1641–1642	1 it.
Land Tax Assessments	1705–1718	47
Lay Subsidies	1568–1600	1 it.
Militia Books	1744–1871	11
Huntingdonshire		
Protestation Returns	1641–1642	1 it.
Kent		
Protestation Returns	1641–1642	1 it.

	Dates Covered	No. of Rolls
Lancashire		
Protestation Returns	1641-1642	1 it.
Leicestershire		
Land Tax Assessments	1773-1832	49
Militia Papers	1667-1883	1
Poll Book	1744	1 it.
Lincolnshire		
Protestation Returns	1641-1642	1 it.
Norfolk		
Lay Subsidies	1598-1640	1 it.
Northumberland		
Protestation Returns	1641-1642	1 it.
Muster Roll	1538	1 it.
Navy Quota Act Returns	1795	1
Returns of Males, 15 to 60 years of age	1798	2
Hair Powder Tax Certificates	1795-1797	1
Poll Book	1698	1
Nottinghamshire		
Protestation Returns	1641-1642	1 it.
Hair Powder Tax Certificates	1795-1798	1 it.
Navy Quota Act Returns	1795	1
Emigration Papers	1819-1820	1
Oxfordshire		
Protestation Returns	1641-1642	1 it.
Land Tax Assessments	1785-1832	33
Militia Minute Books	1778-1862	2
Registration of Lunatics	1832-1854	1
Shropshire		
Protestation Returns	1641-1642	1 it.

	Dates Covered	No. of Rolls
Somerset		
Protestation Returns	1641–1642	1 it.
Lay Subsidies	1624–1674	1
Staffordshire		
Protestation Returns	1641–1642	1 it.
Surrey		
Protestation Returns	1641–1642	1 it.
Poll List for Knights of the Shire	1775	1 it.
Sussex		
Protestation Returns	1641–1642	1 it.
Warwickshire		
Protestation Returns	1641–1642	1 it.
Militia Papers	1780–1847	3
Navy Quota Act Returns	1796–1797	1
Hearth Tax Returns	1662–1684	2
Hair Powder Tax Certificates	1795–1797	1
Register of Electors	1832–1850	6
Penalties Book	1821–1849	1 it.
Lists of High Sheriffs	1161–1935	1
Westmorland		
Protestation Returns	1641–1642	1 it.
Land Tax Assessments	1773–1832	3
Wiltshire		
Protestation Returns	1641–1642	1 it.
Worcestershire		
Protestation Returns	1641–1642	1 it.
Register of Wills Proved in the District Registry	1858–1928	73
Register of Electors, Eastern Division	1843–1888	40

	Dates Covered	No. of Rolls
Yorkshire		
Protestation Returns	1641–1642	2 it.
Land Tax Assessments	1692–1832	65

GOVERNMENT RECORDS: Local

	Dates Covered	No. of Rolls
Berkshire		
Abingdon		
Assessments	1772,1822, 1835	1 it.
Election Certificates	1696-1760	1 it.
Militia Records	1796-1893	1 it.
Aldermaston		
Sunday School Records	1787-1802	1 it.
Aldworth		
School and Clothing Club	1829-1877	1 it.
Yattendon Friendly Society Accounts	1864-1900	1 it.
Bray		
Workhouse Register	1818-1836	1 it.
Biddlestone's Charity	1824-1843	1 it.
Brightwell		
Census Returns	1801-1811	1 it.
Charity Accounts	1723-1836	2 it.
Buckland		
Sunday School Accounts	1789-1806	1 it.
Buscot		
Charity Recipients	1749-1874	1 it.
Coleshill		
Preservation of Peace Order	1779	1 it.
Hagbourne		
Will Book and Charity Records	1688-1769, 1823-1848	2 it
Hurst		
Charity Accounts	1684-1745	1 it.
Ilsley, East		
District Poll Book	1840[5]	1 it.
Lyford		
Clothing Club Records	1857-1875	1

---

[5]The collection includes many printer poll books. Only those which are original manuscripts on microfilm have been inventoried.

	Dates Covered	No. of Rolls
Newbury		
Burgess Roll	1835–1868	1 it.
Charity Accounts	1707–1742	1
Pangbourne		
Census Returns and Valuation List	1801–1896	1 it.
Reading		
Relief of Militiamen's Wives	1793–1811	2 it.
Charity Papers	1621–1887	1
Remenham		
List of Rectors	1297–1784	1 it.
Shinfield		
Charity School Minutes	1824–1834	1 it.
Steventon		
Charity Accounts	1816–1892	1 it.
Thatcham		
Charity School	1794–1859	1 it.
Militia Papers	1780–1821	1 it.
Register of Electors	1854	1 it.
Tilehurst		
Pension Records	1795–1827	1
Ufton Nervet		
Charity Book	1742–1842	1
Wallingford		
Election of Freemen	1734–1802	1 it.
List of Commoners	1788	1 it.
Parliamentary Electors	1832–1833	1 it.
Burgess Roll	1835–1852	1 it.
Waltham St. Lawrence		
Militia Orders	1794–1810	1 it.
Wantage		
List of Persons in Workhouse	1757	1 it.
Warfield		
Charity Accounts	1748–1886	1 it.
List of Incumbents	1290–1901	1 it.
Voting Papers for Guardians of the Poor	1616–1836	1 it.
Wokingham		
Charity Accounts	1649–1836	1 it.
Admission of Freemen	1708–1869	1 it.

	Dates Covered	No. of Rolls
Buckinghamshire		
Aylesbury		
Land Tax	1780–1830	4
Poll Books	1722–1857	4
Olney		
National School	1819–1823	1 it.
Cambridgeshire		
Soham		
Apprenticeship Lists	1844–1861	2 it.
Witchford		
Militia Enrollment Records	1782–1831	3
Cheshire		
Broxton		
Register of Electors	1832–1841	4 it.
Bucklow Hill		
Register of Electors	1832–1841	4 it.
Chester		
A List of Voters	1812	1 it.
Register of Electors	1832–1841	5 it.
Sheriff's Poll Books	1837,1841	2 it.
Congleton		
Sheriff's Poll Book	1841	1 it.
Eddisbury		
Register of Electors	1832–1841	4 it.
Macclesfield		
Register of Electors	1832–1841	5 it.
Sheriff's Poll Book	1841	1 it.
Malpas		
Sheriff's Poll Books	1837,1841	2 it.
Mottram in Longdendale		
Sheriff's Poll Book	1841	1 it.
Nantwich		
Register of Electors	1832–1841	5 it.
Sheriff's Poll Books	1837,1841	2 it.
Northwich		
Register of Electors	1832–1841	5 it.
Sheriff's Poll Books	1837,1841	2 it.
Runcorn		
Register of Electors	1832	1
Sheriff's Poll Book	1841	1 it.

	Dates Covered	No. of Rolls
Sandbach		
Sheriff's Poll Books	1837,1841	2 it.
Stockport		
Land Tax Assessment	1780	1
Register of Electors	1832	1
Sheriff's Poll Book	1841	1 it.
Cornwall		
Bodmin		
Receipts and Expenses in Building Bodmin Church	1469–1472	1
Laneast		
Register of Services	1921–1954	1
Tywardreath		
Registrum Commun	1504–1519	1 it.
Cumberland		
Bewcastle		
School Records	1855–1905	1
Carlisle		
Joint Burial Board, Burial Records, Indexed	1855–1899	19
Derbyshire		
Pleasley		
Minutes of School Managers' Meetings	1884–1900	1 it.
Devonshire		
Exeter		
The List of the Freemen of the City of Exeter entitled to Vote in the Election	1859,1860	1
A List of Voters for Exeter	1859	1 it.
Dorsetshire		
Cattistock		
Register of Births, Marriages, Deaths	1839	1 it.
Durham		
Durham		
Poll Books	1820–1863	3 it.
County Polls	1675–1680, 1722	1
City Polls	1678–1679	1
Sunderland		
Election Registers	1841–1868, 1874	1
Burgess Lists	1870–1892	4

	Dates Covered	No. of Rolls
Essex		
Colchester		
Poll for the Borough	1830	1 it.
Havering Levels		2
Freeholders List	1795	
Presentment Book	1739-1762	
Pool Book, Hair Powder Tax List, Indexed	1694-1695	
Gloucestershire		
Dymock		
Register of Churchwardens and Parish Officers	1595-1792	1
Benefactions to the Poor	1768-1851	1 it.
Ann Cam's Charity School	1785-1870	2 it.
Gloucester		
Ward Lists and Election Registers	1843-1886	8
"The Gloucester Journal"	1731-1802	16
Henbury		
Tithes	1642-1802	1 it.
Hertfordshire		
Ashwell		
Militia Papers	1810	1 it.
Hadham, Much		
Workhouse Committee Minutes and Correspondence	1833-1835	1 it.
Hitchin		
Charity Records	1734-1872	1 it.
Militia Records	1803-1806	3
Surveyor's Lists	1809-1834	1 it.
Hoddesdon		
Voters' Certificates	1832,1839	1 it.
Kings Langley		
Charities	1786-1868	1
Royston		
Servant and Apprentice Papers	1784-1809	1 it.
Thundridge		
Charities	1658-1695	1 it.
Ware		
Voters' Certificates	1832-1835	1 it.
Kent		
Cranbrook		
Free Grammar School Estates	1808-1812	1

	Dates Covered	No. of Rolls
Lancashire		
Ashton-Under-Lyne		
Teacher's Day Book	1863-1891	1 it.
Croston		
School Board Minutes	1878-1890	1 it.
Land Valuation	1806-1828	1 it.
Rent Rolls, Terriers	1723-1828	1 it.
Kirkham		
Charities	1904	1 it.
Liverpool		
Henry Park, Surgeon, and His Register of Births, Indexed	1769-1830	1 it.
Padiham		
Civil Register of Births	1842-1849	1 it.
Census	1841	1 it.
Leicestershire		
Swithland		
Field Tythes	1764-1814	1 it.
Lincolnshire		
Kirby Underwood		
The Towne Book of Kirby Underwood	1616-1904	1 it.
Lincoln and Kesteven		
Hearth Tax Returns, Indexed	1665-1671	1
Norfolk		
Coltishall and Horstead with Stanninghall		
Village Surveys	1564,1584, 1586	3 it.
Forehoe Hundred		
Militia Muster Roll	1714	1 it.
Lessingham with Hempstead		
Village Surveys	1584	1 it.
Norwich		
Contested Elections	1780	1 it.
Poll Books and Electoral Records	1714-1799	1
Poll Books	1806-1870	1
Taverham Deanery		
Land Tax Assessments	1781,1782, 1789	1
Thorpe next Norwich		
Rosary Burial Grant	1821-1837	1 it.

	Dates Covered	No. of Rolls
Toft Monks		
Village Survey	1566	1 it.
Yarmouth, Great		
Poll Books	1754-1865	1
Northumberland		
Benwell Township		
Parish Census, 6 June - 23 July	1860	1 it.
Berwick upon Tweed		
Guild Books	1504-1833	19
Employment Register	1816-1817	1
Roll Book of Freemen	1752-1875	1
List of Apprentices	1807-1867	1
Parish Casual Books	1812-1835	4
Constable's Return of Male Residents Aged 18 to 45	1819	1
Burial Grant Books	1856-1948	5
Haltwhistle		
Lady Capel's Will and Charity	1718	1 it.
Newcastle upon Tyne		
Mayors, Bailiffs, and Sheriffs;	1251-1742	
Vicars;	1374-1728	
Governors of Merchant Companies	1546-1739	1
Common Council Act Books	1656-1722	1
Poll Book	1722-1723	1 it.
Petitions to the Common Council	1728-1850	1
Freemen Admission Book	1733-1839	2
Alphabetical List, Index to Guild Book of Freemen	1738-1775	1
Land Tax for Various Parishes and Wards	1747-1872	10
Lay Subsidy Roll	1326	1 it.
Land Tax Assessments	1748-1830	1
Ward List of Burgesses	1835-1878	9
Poll Book, St. Andrews Ward	1836, 1870-1871	1
Electors' Register	1863-1879	5
Citizens' Roll, Street Indexed	1882-1900	27
Grants of Grave Spaces	1858-1900	6
St. John's Parish--Lists of Parish Officers	1760-1824	1 it.
St. John's Parish--Vestry Meetings	1769-1824	1 it.
Loyal Newcastle Associated Volunteer Infantry Meetings	1808-1813	1 it.
Nottinghamshire		
Balderton		
Charities	1786	1 it.
Barnby in the Willows		
Register of Burials in Woolen	1678-1734	1 it.
Bilborough		
Tax Assessments	1781	1 it.

	Dates Covered	No. of Rolls
Bleasby		
List of Householders and Church Seatings	1876	1 it.
Particulars of Bleasby Lordship	1777	1 it.
Farnsfield		
List of Church Scholars	1789	1 it.
Gamston		
Tax Assessments	1789–1799	1 it.
Marnham		
Charity Account Book	1695–1880	1 it.
Newark		
Canvas of Newark	1790	1
Disputed Election Poll Books	1787–1795	1 it.
Register of Electors	1832–1846	1
Burgess Roll	1835–1853	1 it.
Norwell		
Militia List	1797	1 it.
List of Inhabitants	1798	1 it.
Nottingham		
Apprentice Register, Indexed	1723–1846	2
Subscription Book for the Duke of Kensington's Light Horse	1745	1 it.
Strelley		
Land and Window Tax Assessments; Appointment of Tax Collector	1750–1766	3 it.
Sutton		
Names of Parish Officers	1637–1870	1 it.
Thorpe		
Land Tax Assessments	1818,1822	1 it.
Tax Collectors' Papers	1815–1823	1 it.

Oxfordshire

	Dates Covered	No. of Rolls
Banbury		
Banbury Union Poor Law Minute Book	1839–1900	15
Freemasons' Annual Returns, Cherwell Lodge	1860–1875[6]	1 it.
Bicester		
Bicester Union Poor Law Minute Book	1835–1900	13
Chipping Norton		
Chipping Norton Union Poor Law Minute Book	1837–1900	6
Freemasons' Annual Returns, Bowyer Lodge	1868–1875	1 it.

---

[6]Returns of Freemasons are made by local government units to the Commissions of the Peace at quarter sessions. Some returns are also cataloged under Commissions of the Peace and some under quarter sessions.

	Dates Covered	No. of Rolls
Henley-on-Thames		
Henley Union Poor Law Minute Book	1835-1900	8
Oxford		
Freemasons' Annual Returns, Apollo Lodge	1834-1874	1 it.
Alfred Lodge	1834-1875	1 it.
Bertie Lodge	1875	1 it.
Thame		
Thame Union Poor Law Minute Book	1835-1900	10
Woodstock		
Woodstock Union Poor Law Minute Book	1835-1900	10
Freemasons' Annual Returns, Marlborough Lodge	1872-1875	1 it.
Staffordshire		
Upper Arley		
Endowment of site to build school	1859	1 it.
Surrey		
Chipstead		
Apportionment of the Rent Charte in lieu of Tithes	1847	1 it.
Guildford		
Poll Books and Registers	1796-1843	2
Warwickshire		
Alcester		
Apprenticeship Registers	1677-1860	1
Coleshill		
Census Records	1811,1821, 1831	1
Elmdon		
School Accounts	1858-1876	1 it.
Grandborough		
Enclosure Accounts	1623,1760, 1766	1 it.
Kenilworth		
School Accounts and Minutes	1846-1900	1
Lapworth		
Charity Accounts	1837-1848	1
Leamington Hastings		
Charity and Legal Papers	1771-1892	1
Mancetter		
Correspondence and Legal Papers	1750-1752	1 it.

	Dates Covered	No. of Rolls
Oxhill		
Charity Account Book	1833-1864	1 it.
Pillerton Priors		
Apprentice Register	1805-1833	1 it.
Polesworth		
Sir Francis Nethersole's Charity School	1559-1929	2
Sheldon		
List of Males	1845	1 it.
Shustoke		
Apprentice Book	1802-1830	1 it.
Tanworth		
Register of Houses	1826-1888	1 it.
Charity Accounts	1738-1881	1 it.
Temple Balsall		
Lady Katherine Leveson's Hospital	1632-1821	2
Warwick		
Robert, Earl of Leicester's Hospital Records	1616-1903	9
City Charity and Apprenticeship Records	1546-1888	14
St. Mary's Parish Charity and Apprentice-ship Records	1705-1868	4
St. Nicholas' Parish Charity and Apprentice-ship Records	1672-1913	4
Wellesbourne Hastings		
School Log Books	1876-1930	1
Wootten Wawen		
Village Survey	1589	1 it.
Westmorland		
Kendal		
Workhouse Documents	1836-1914	1
Preston Richard		
List of Freeholders	1818-1825	1 it.
List of Innkeepers	1825	1 it.
Wiltshire		
Ogbourne		
Village Survey	1246	1 it.
Worcestershire		
Abberley		
Register of Apprentices	1808-1822	1 it.
Alvechurch		
School Accounts and Minutes	1894-1920	2 it.

	Dates Covered	No. of Rolls
Evesham		
Poll Book for the Borough of Evesham	1780	1 it.
Himbleton		
Account of Population (Census)	1821	1 it.
Kidderminster		
A List of Residents in Kidderminster	1889	1
School Records	1903-1951	3
Census Books	1801,1811 1831	1 it.
Kings Pyon		
School Records	1873-1954	2 it.
Lindridge		
School Manager's Minute Book	1870-1951	1
Apprenticeship Register	1828-1951	1 it.
Overbury		
Church of England School Log Book	1907-1966	1 it.
Pershore		
Charity Account Book	1880-1939	1 it.
Ripple		
Charity Accounts	1789-1850	1 it.
Rock		
School Account Book	1862-1869	1 it.
Shelsley Beauchamp		
Webbs Charity Minute Book	1932-1968	1
Stockton-on-Teme		
Reading Room Members Register and Minutes	1889-1924	1 it.
Wichenford		
Apprenticeship Papers	1769-1829	1 it.
Wolverley		
Population Book of Wolverley	1814-1834	2
Worcester		
Charity Records	1718-1821	1
Royal Grammar School--Accounts and Records	1561-1895	5
St. Oswald's Hospital--Vital Records and Accounts	1600-1964	13
St. Andrew's Parish--Charity Papers	to 1912	2 it.
St. Clement's Parish--Charity Accounts and Correspondence	1882-1948	2 it.

Yorkshire

	Dates Covered	No. of Rolls
Crofton		
Militia List for the Township of Crofton	1824	1 it.

	Dates Covered	No. of Rolls
Mirfield		
Militia List for the Township of Mirfield	1825	1 it.
Richmond		
Borough Coucher Books	1752–1832	1
Pontefract		
Fee Farm and Burgage Rents	1767	1 it.

II LEGAL RECORDS

LEGAL RECORDS: National

	Dates Covered	No. of Rolls
CHANCERY		
Papers		
Proceedings, Series I, C. 2	1603-1625	1
Indexes		
Calendar of Chancery Proceedings, C. 6	1625-1714	7
Calendar of Chancery Proceedings, C. 7-10	before 1714	18
Calendar of Chancery Proceedings, C. 11	1714-1758	10
Calendar of Chancery Proceedings, C. 12	1758-1800	10
Calendar of Chancery Proceedings, C. 13	1800-1842	5
Calendar of Miscellaneous Proceedings, C. 18	1662 - 19th C.	1
Calendar of Country Depositions, C. 21-22	1649-1714	5
Calendar of Town Depositions, C. 24	1534-1558	1
Guide to Charity Petitions, C. 29	1836-1845	1
List of Affidavits, C. 31	1611-1875	1
List of Chancery Cause Books, C. 32	1842-1880	1
Guide to Ordinary and Appeal Petitions, C. 36	1774-1851	1
Registrars' Minute Books, C. 37	1639-1875	1
Calendar of Indentures Enrolled in Close Rolls, C. 54	1574-1860	26
Calendar of Grantees Enrolled on the Close Rolls, C. 54	1461-1848	50
Guide to Decree Rolls, C. 78-79	1534-1903	6
Calendar of Masters' Reports and Certificates, C. 38	1544-1875	1
Index to Chancery Proceedings	1758-1800	4

	Dates Covered	No. of Rolls
COMMON PLEAS		
Indexes		
Records of Attorneys and Solicitors, Index to Articles of Clerkship, C.P. 5	1725–1838	1
Calendar of Final Concords, Land Registration and Feet of Fines (Lincolnshire)	1272–1603	10
Feet of Fines (various counties)	1509–1521	1
Feet of Fines (Northumberland)	1514–1603	1
Feet of Fines Deforciants	1635	1
EXCHEQUER		
Papers		
Inquisitions Post Mortem (Exeter)	1300–1600	7
Indexes		
Calendarium Inquisitionum Post Mortem sive Escaetarum	1806	1 it.
Exchequer Deponents (Cornwall, Devon, Dorset, Somerset)	1558–1664	1

LEGAL RECORDS: County

	Dates Covered	No. of Rolls
ASSIZES[1]		
Papers		
Buckinghamshire		
Sheriff's Jury Books	1769-1800	1
Cheshire		
Death Warrants and Reprieves	1801-1852	5
Northumberland		
Transportation orders	1768-1834	1
Indexes		
Oxfordshire		
Calendar of Depositions	1567-1578	1
COMMISSIONS OF THE PEACE[2]		
Papers		
Berkshire	1703-1868	17
Buckinghamshire	1718-1852	28
Cambridgeshire	1660-1852	11
Conveyance of Vagrants	1701-1832	1
Durham	1616-1883	28
Essex		
Jurors' Books	1838-1848	1
Hereford	1655-1915	15
Hertfordshire	1631-1689	1
Lancashire	1626-1888	78

---

[1]Some assize records are incorrectly cataloged as quarter sessions.

[2]No attempt was made to itemize all quarter sessions papers beyond existing catalog information. The most common records are correspondence (in and out), order books, minute books, jury books, recognizances, presentments and indictments, and oaths of Papists. The library also has most of the quarter sessions records printed by local record societies.

	Dates Covered	No. of Rolls
Leicestershire	1607–1795	26
Northumberland	1649–1875	55
Returns of Papists	1706–1745	1
Nottinghamshire	1452–1904	158
Oxfordshire	1689–1925	34
Somerset	1613–1891	61
Suffolk	1639–1782	12
Surrey	1698–1901	2
Warwickshire	1661–1889	144
Returns of Names and Addresses of the Acting County Magistrates	1824–1869	1
Westmorland		
Jury Lists	1775–1844	1
Papists Estates	1717	1
Worcestershire	1693–1960	42
Yorkshire		
North Riding	1605–1881	49
Juror's Books	1729–1848	6
Southwell including Scrooby, Nottinghamshire	1603–1837	8

Registers

Quarter Sessions Records available at the
Genealogical Society of Utah, 1 vol.

DEEDS AND LEGAL INSTRUMENTS

Papers

	Dates Covered	No. of Rolls
Buckinghamshire		
Abstracts of Deeds	1582–1811	1
Cheshire		
Accounts and Receipts for Conveyance of Vagrants	1701–1832	1
Cornwall		
Abstracts of Deeds, Indexed	1700–1800	1
Oxfordshire		
Transcripts of Indentures	1614–1731	1
Somerset		
Estate Duty Wills	1812–1857	97

	Dates Covered	No. of Rolls
Suffolk		
Abstracts of Deeds	17th – 18th C.	1
Warwickshire		
Inclosure Awards[3]	1692–1850	4
Worcestershire		
Inclosure Awards	1763–1830	2
Tuition Bonds and Acts of Guardianship	1685–1814	2
Yorkshire		
North Riding, Registry of Deeds.		
Deeds, Wills and Conveyances	1736–1876	167

Indexes

	Dates Covered	No. of Rolls
Surrey		
Calendar of Deeds, Indexed	17th – 18th C.	14
Warwickshire		
Calendar of Deeds	1612–1889	1
Yorkshire		
Healaugh, Registry of Deeds, Mortgage Register	1823–1892	1

---

[3]Inclosure awards and registration of Papist estates are also found in quarter session papers.

LEGAL RECORDS: Local

	Dates Covered	No. of Rolls
COURT RECORDS		
Bedfordshire		
Biggleswade		
Court Records	1540-1858	2
Berkshire		
Abingdon		
Borough Court Records	1650-1839	4
Ashbury		
Manor Court Rolls	1572-1841	1 it.
Blewbury		
Manor Court Books	1665-1938	4
Brimpton		
Manor Court Rolls	1347-1786	2
Cookham		
Manor Court Rolls, Indexed	1689-1851	4
Easthampstead		
Constables' Orders	1766-1858	1 it.
Enbourne		
Manor Court Rolls	1663-1841	1 it.
Faringdon, Great		
Manor Court Books	1737-1859	4
Hampstead Marshall		
Manor Court Rolls	1668-1840	1
Hungerford		
Coroners' Court Inquisitions	1813-1877	1
Hurst		
Manor Court Books	1600-1930	2
Ilsley, East		
Ashridge Manor Court Books	1621-1754	1
Inkpen		
Manor Court Records	1300-1840	1
Kintbury		
Manor Court Rolls	1663-1840	1 it.

	Dates Covered	No. of Rolls
Newbury		
Court Leet Presentments	1799–1877	2
Shaw		
Manor Court Rolls	1405–1529	1
Shrivenham		
Manor Court Books	1523–1862	12
Speen		
Manor Court Rolls	1562–1838	1
Uffington		
Manor Court Books	1720–1811	1 it.
Wallingford		
Coroners' Court Records	1291–1319	1 it.
Keepers of the Peace	1308–1320	1 it.
Oath Rolls	1709–1827	1 it.
Borough Court Records	1227–1852	4

Cambridgeshire

	Dates Covered	No. of Rolls
Bassingbourn		
Manor Court Book	1709–1852	3
Bottisham		
Manor Court Records	1736–1881	1 it.
Burrough Green		
Manor Court Book	1648–1792	1 it.
Burwell		
Manor Court Records	1733–1879	2
Cheveley		
Manor Court Book	1736–1849	1
Chippenham		
Manor Court Book	1685–1742	1 it.
Comberton Greenes		
Manor Court Records	1617–1876	2
Coton		
Manor Court Records	1736–1866	1
Cottenham		
Manor Court Records	1703–1866	4
Coveney		
Manor Court Books	1660–1850	6
Docwraies		
Manor Court Books	1502–1880	1
Elsworth		
Manor Court Books	1767–1851	1

	Dates Covered	No. of Rolls
Fordham		
Manor Court Records	1693–1878	1
Foxton		
Manor Court Records	1709–1896	3
Fulbourn		
Manor Court Records	1700–1853	2
Haddenham		
Manor Court Records	1643–1852	6
Harston		
Manor Court Books	1729–1848	2
Haslingfield		
Manor Court Books	1729–1854	1
Hildersham		
Manor Court Books	1748–1817	1 it.
Histon		
Manor Court Books	1701–1862	6
Horningsen		
Manor Court Books	1684–1845	1 it.
Ickleton		
Manor Court Books	1774–1851	1 it.
Isleham		
Manor Court Books	1673–1883	3
Kingston		
Manor Court Books	1805–1863	1
Landbeach		
Manor Court Books	1822–1851	1 it.
Linton		
Manor Court Books	1661–1813	2
Littleport		
Manor Court Books	1624–1858	7
Meldreth		
Manor Court Records	1782–1847	1 it.
Milton		
Manor Court Books	1651–1718	1 it.
Netherhall Wygorne		
Manor Court Records	1690–1868	2
Over		
Court Rolls	1729–1779	1
Manor Court Books	1729–1851	4

	Dates Covered	No. of Rolls
Shepreth		
Manor Court Rolls	1708-1868	1 it.
Shudy Camps		
Manor Court Books	1727-1884	2 it.
Soham		
Manor Court Books	1694-1852	8
Stapleford		
Manor Court Rolls	1661-1823	2
Stetchworth		
Manor Court Books	1787-1874	3
Stuntney		
Manor Court Books	1741-1829	1
Swaffham Bulbeck		
Manor Court Books	1666-1851	1
Swaffham Prior		
Manor Court Books	1673-1875	2
Swavesey		
Manor Court Books	1753-1860	2
Thetford		
Manor Court Rolls	1702-1851	3
Trumpington		
Manor Court Books	1764-1856	1 it.
Whittlesey		
Court Rolls, Indexed	1612-1728	4
Wicken		
Manor Court Records	1764-1858	2
Willingham		
Manor Court Books	1614-1852	4
Wood Ditton		
Manor Court Books	1665-1851	5
Wratting, West		
Manor Court Books	1822-1851	1 it.

Devon

Exeter		
A List of the Clerks of the quarter sessions	1352-1971	
Clerks of the Peace	1537-1971	
Sheriffs	1765-1971	1 it.

	Dates Covered	No. of Rolls
Dorset		
Corfe Castle and Kingston Court Records	1578–1762	3
Great Canford and Poole Court Books	1723–1850	2
Herefordshire		
Orleton Manor Records	1623–1849	2
Lancashire		

Liverpool
    House of Correction. List of Female Convicts
       under Sentence of Transportation
	1838	1 it.

Norfolk		
Buckenham with Mannington, Itteringham Manor Court Rolls	1562–1730	1 it.
Martham Manor Court Books	1678–1797	2 it.
Northumberland		
Anick Grange Manor Records	1627–1839	3
Berwick upon Tweed Court Records	1598–1828	47
Quarter Sessions Books of the Borough	1727–1781	2
Constables' Returns of Male Residents (18 to 45)	1819	1
Hexham Manor Records	1558–1872	18
Newcastle upon Tyne Calendar of Prisoners	1736	1
Mayor's Court	1649–1719	16
Nonconformist Oaths and Declarations	1685–1824	1
Sheriff's Court	1613–1685	9
Spittal Manor Court Books of Tweedmouth and Spittal	1658–1857	4
Tynemouth Manor Court Admissions	1836–1849	1

	Dates Covered	No. of Rolls
Nottinghamshire		
Cropwell Butler		
Order to Southwell House of Correction	1735	1 it.
Laneham		
Court Book	1614-1629	1 it.
Norwell		
Constable's Records	1794-1836	1 it.
Nottingham		
Quarter Sessions Rolls for the City of Nottingham	1498-1827	31
Ollerton		
Orders to Constables	1622, 1664	1 it.
Strelley		
Constable's Levies	1756-1764	1 it.
Oxfordshire		
Minster Lovell		
Court Rolls	1560-1627	1
Shropshire		
Ellesmere Manor		
Court Book	1734-1841	1 it.
Index to Manorial Court Grants	1630-1857	1 it.
Surrey		
Guildford		
Quarter Sessions Minute Books	1698-1901	2
Warwickshire		
Coventry		
Adjourned Records of the Warwick Quarter Sessions	1718-1852	11
Warwick		
Book of John Fisher, Bailiff of Warwick	1580-1588	1
Westmorland		
Preston Richard		
Court Book	1678-1747	1 it.
Yorkshire		
Alne		
Manor Court Book	1737-1901	1
Barningham		
Manor Court Book	1783-1841	1

	Dates Covered	No. of Rolls
Easingwold Manor Court Book	1719-1891	1
Haxby Manor Court Books	1679-1886	3
Healaugh and Muker Manor Court Books	1686-1879	6
Husthwaite Manor Court Books	1817-1875	1
Northallerton Manor Court Books	1662-1884	15
Osbaldwick Manor Court Books and Land Records	1670-1887	3
Strensell Manor Court Book	1828-1876	2
Thirsk Manor Court Book	1622-1790	2

DEEDS AND LEGAL INSTRUMENTS

Berkshire

	Dates Covered	No. of Rolls
Abingdon Indentures	1768,1825, 1881	1 it.
Apprenticeship Indentures	1633-1793	1 it.
Binfield Charity Deeds and Accounts	1648-1902	2 it.
Blewbury Apprenticeship Papers	1704-1780	2 it.
Bray Apprenticeship Papers	1658-1817	1 it.
Brightwell Apprenticeship Indentures	1753-1824	1 it.
Burghfield Apprenticeship Indentures	1713-1808	1 it.
Buscot Terrier of Lands	1837-1884	1 it.
Chieveley Bonds and Indentures	1707-1830	2 it.
Coleshill Apprenticeship Indentures	1763-1768	1 it.

	Dates Covered	No. of Rolls
Drayton		
Affidavits for Burials and Coroners' Certificates	1778-1823	1 it.
Englefield		
Apprenticeship Indentures	1663-1795	1 it.
Hungerford		
Register Book of Apprentices and Freemen	1582-1777	1
Hurst		
Apprenticeship Indentures	1685-1783	1 it.
Newbury		
Apprenticeship Indentures	1784-1813	1 it.
Reading		
Apprenticeship Indentures	1643-1852	1 it.
Shellingford		
Deeds and Indentures	1778-1827	1 it.
Shinfield		
Apprenticeship Indentures	1654-1822	1 it.
Thatcham		
Apprenticeship Indentures	1671-1818	1 it.
Tilehurst		
Apprenticeship Records	1700-1900	1
Wallingford		
Apprenticeship Indentures	1610-1711	1 it.
Wantage		
Apprenticeship Papers	1678-1800	1 it.
Loan Agreements	1700-1786	1 it.
Warfield		
Apprenticeship Indentures	1663-1800	1 it.

Cheshire

	Dates Covered	No. of Rolls
Chester		
Prison Records and Orders	1806-1857	5

Cornwall

	Dates Covered	No. of Rolls
Lanreath		
Apprenticeship Records	1726-1837	2 it.
Bonds and Indentures	1664-1824	1 it.
Sheviock		
Apprenticeship Records	1744-1837	2 it.

	Dates Covered	No. of Rolls
Cumberland		
Cumwhitton		
Bastardy Orders	1823–1841	1 it.
Royston		
Servant and Apprenticeship Papers	1784–1809	1 it.
Hampshire		
Liphook		
Foley Manor, Deed Extracts		1 it.
Hertfordshire		
Ashwell		
Bastardy Bonds	1713–1834	1 it.
Apprenticeship Papers	1726–1863	1 it.
Barkway		
Apprenticeship and Bastardy Papers	1629–1842	1 it.
Bishop's Stortford		
Apprenticeship Papers	1598–1790	1 it.
Cheshunt		
Apprenticeship Papers	1615–1815	1 it.
Datchworth		
Apprenticeship and Bastardy Papers	1700–1840	1 it.
Essenden		
Apprenticeship Papers	1659–1854	1 it.
Gaddesden, Great		
Apprenticeship Papers	1685–1823	1 it.
Hertford		
Apprenticeship and Bastardy Papers	1669–1806	1 it.
Hitchin		
Apprenticeship Papers	17th – 19th C.	1
Hoddesden		
Apprenticeship and Bastardy Papers	1688–1845	1
Kings Langley		
Apprenticeship and Bastardy Papers	1677–1826	2 it.
Royston		
Apprenticeship and Bastardy Papers	1712–1824	2 it.
St. Albans		
Apprenticeship and Bastardy Papers	1683–1830	3 it.

	Dates Covered	No. of Rolls
Watford Bastardy Bonds	1810-1821	1 it.
Lancashire		
Bickerstaffe Apprenticeship Papers	1716-1824	1 it.
Burscough Apprenticeship Papers	1692-1832	1 it.
Cronton Apprenticeship Papers	1719-1835	1 it.
Harwood, Great Apprenticeship Papers	1723-1819	1 it.
Kirkham Apprenticeship Papers	1705-1838	1 it.
Lowton Apprenticeship Papers	1784-1830	1 it.
Manchester Apprenticeship Indentures	1800-1830	1
Simonswood Apprenticeship Papers	1728-1829	1 it.
Norfolk		
Hunworth Deeds	1727-1834	1 it.
Northumberland		

Berwick upon Tweed
    Apprenticeship Indentures
    List of Apprentices Serving for Freedom
	1713-1872
	1807-1867
		1
		1

Newcastle upon Tyne
    Deeds in Durham Treasury
    Topographical Card Index to Deeds
	
	14th -
	19th C.
		1
		5

Nottinghamshire		
Balderton Bonds	1735	2 it.
Barton in Farbis Articles of Agreement	1718,1729, 1766	1 it.
Bilsthorpe Apprenticeship Indentures	1839	1 it.

	Dates Covered	No. of Rolls
Bleasby		
Bonds and Indentures	1701-1908	2 it.
Blidworth		
Bonds and Indentures	1764-1821	3 it.
Cotgrave		
Bonds and Indentures	1758-1800	1 it.
Drayton, East		
Return of Jurors	1814	1 it.
Eakring		
Bastardy Bonds	1768	1 it.
Eastwood		
Warrant, Presentments, Bonds and Certificates	1707-1835	1 it.
Egmanton		
Bastardy Bonds	1705-1843	1 it.
Elkesley		
Apprenticeship Indentures	1697-1700	1 it.
Agreements	1682-1768	1 it.
Keyworth		
Bonds and Indentures	1731-1801	2 it.
Laxton		
Apprenticeship Indentures and Bastardy Papers	1683-1848	3 it.
Leake, East		
Bastardy Bonds	1783-1825	1 it.
Servants Registers	1818-1833	1 it.
Leverton, South		
Bastardy Bonds	1787-1822	1 it.
Mission		
Bonds and Indentures	1650-1806	3 it.
Norwell		
Indemnity Bonds	1803-1806	1 it.
Ollerton		
Bastardy Orders and Bonds	1688-1808	2 it.
Apprenticeship Indentures	1665-1825	1 it.
Inventories and Memorands	1689-1861	1 it.
Rempstone		
Apprenticeship Indentures	1731-1829	1 it.
Ruddington		
Indentures, Bonds and Agreements	1674-1900	2
Shelford		
Apprenticeship Indentures	1686-1840	1

	Dates Covered	No. of Rolls
Strelley		
Apprenticeship Indentures	1713–1777	1 it.
Bastardy Bonds	1734–1776	1 it.
Syerston		
Bastardy Records, Sheriff Summons and Schoolmasters' Licenses		3 it.
Upton		
Apprenticeship Indentures and Bastardy Bonds	1749–1816	3 it.
Suffolk		
Ipswich		
Apprenticeship Indentures	1596–1651	1 it.
Warwickshire		
Barford		
Charity Deeds	1553–1746	1 it.
Baxterley		
Apprenticeship Indentures	1806–1907	1 it.
Bedworth		
Charity Deeds	1766–1940	1
Bickenhill		
Enclosure Awards	1824,1843 1845	1
Bramcote		
Apprenticeship Indentures	1660–1831	1 it.
Burdingbury		
Deeds	1733–1763	1 it.
Claverdon		
Charity Deeds	1556–1848	2
Emscote		
Deeds	1872	1 it.
Exhall		
Apprenticeship Indentures	1689–1873	1 it.
Idlecote		
Deeds	1556–1812	1 it.
Kineton		
Deeds	1820–1875	1 it.
Knowle		
Deeds and Indentures	1641–1895	3 it.
Meriden		
Deeds	1843	1 it.

	Dates Covered	No. of Rolls
Napton on the Hill Charity Deeds	1639-1875	1 it.
Nether Whitacre Enclosures and Indentures	1627-1878	1 it.
Nuneaton Apprenticeship Indentures	1774-1875	2
Packwood Conveyances	1817-1862	1 it.
Polesworth Indentures	1643-1846	2
Sheldon Apprenticeship Indentures	1715-1833	1 it.
Shustoke Bonds and Indentures	1671-1812	1 it.
Snitterfield Charity Deeds	17th - 18th C.	1 it.
Deeds	1823-1825	1 it.
Solihull Charity Deeds	1538-1907	3
Southam Deeds	1360-1567	1
Stockingford Deeds	1859-1890	1
Sutton Coldfield Enclosure Award	1851	1
Tanworth Apprenticeship Indentures	17th- 18th C.	1
Warwick St. Nicholas Charity Deeds	1655-1875	1 it.
Weddington Deeds	1807-1845	1
Whitacre (Over) Charity Deeds	1853-1877	1

	Dates Covered	No. of Rolls
Worcestershire		
Abberley		
Apprenticeship Indentures	19th C.	1 it.
Alvechurch		
Apprenticeship Records	18th–19th C.	1
Badsey		
Apprenticeship Indentures	1759–1803	1 it.
Besford		
Bastardy Papers	1775–1810	1 it.
Broadway		
Bastardy Papers and Bonds	1651–1878	4 it.
Chaddesley Corbett		
Apprenticeship Indentures	17th–19th C.	1
Church Honeybourne		
Enclosure Award	1778	1 it.
Claines, North		
Apprenticeship Indentures	1606–1826	3
Cofton Hackett		
Apprenticeship Papers	1811–1818	1 it.
Droitwich		
Apprenticeship Papers	1700–1826	2
Feckenham		
Bastardy Accounts	1836–1838	1 it.
Hartlebury		
Bastardy Bonds	1750–1850	1 it.
Himbleton		
Apprenticeships	1799–1805	1 it.
Longdon		
Bonds and Indentures	1697–1796	2 it.
Martley		
Apprenticeship Indentures	1699–1767	1 it.
Ombersley		
Apprenticeship and Bastardy Papers	17th–19th C.	2
Ripple		
Apprenticeship Indentures	1636–1834	1

	Dates Covered	No. of Rolls
Stone		
Charity Deeds and Papers	to 1910	2
Worcester		
St. Clement, School Deeds	19th C.	1 it.
St. Swithin, Apprenticeship Indentures	17th-18th C.	1 it.

III CHURCH RECORDS

The section on church records contains documents made by several church authorities in England and kept in the archives of these various church authorities. The principal class is of course the Church of England, and there is another category for Nonconformist churches. The records of the British L.D.S. Mission are located in the Archives of the L.D.S. Church Historical Department. Some have been microfilmed for the Genealogical Society's library. Dating from 1830, these include membership, emigration and historical records. Two printed guides written by Laureen R. Jaussi and Gloria D. Chaston (published by Deseret Book Company, Salt Lake City, Utah) provide a full listing of these records: Genealogical Records of Utah, 1974 and 1977; and Registers of L.D.S. Church Records, 1968. Copies of these are available for use in the Society's library.

Within the section on church records, the material is limited to cases where the church authority prepared, sanctioned, and filed a legal record. Thus records of marriage and probate are the principal classes, and to them are added some incidental ecclesiastical records. Other parochial documents are treated as Government Records - Local.

Church of England records are listed here by diocese, and the specific date of diocesan boundaries used is 1830. The most efficient classification for genealogical research in church records is the geographic, county orientation. Thus the Society's catalog is principally arranged by counties, although persons using the catalog should consult both county and diocesan entries. The present Inventory, however, is aimed at researchers in general and as its organization is by provenance, and there are already guides to church records by county, the diocesan division will be used here. To assist researchers, the following County-Diocese key is provided:

COUNTY-DIOCESE

County	Diocese
Bedfordshire	Lincoln
Berkshire	Salisbury
Buckinghamshire	Lincoln
Cambridgeshire	Ely, Norwich
Cheshire	Chester
Cornwall	Exeter
Cumberland	Carlisle, Chester
Derbyshire	Lichfield & Coventry
Devon	Exeter
Dorset	Bristol
Durham	Durham
Essex	London
Gloucestershire	Gloucester Bristol
Hampshire	Winchester
Herefordshire	Hereford
Hertfordshire	Lincoln, London
Huntingdonshire	Lincoln
Kent	Canterbury, Rochester
Lancashire	Chester
Leicestershire	Lincoln
Lincolnshire	Lincoln
London	London
Norfolk	Norwich
Northamptonshire	Peterborough
Northumberland	Durham
Nottinghamshire	York
Oxford	Oxford
Rutlandshire	Peterborough
Shropshire	Hereford, Lichfield & Coventry
Somersetshire	Bath & Wells
Staffordshire	Lichfield & Coventry
Suffolk	Norwich
Surrey	Winchester
Sussex	Chichester
Warwickshire	Worcester, Lichfield & Coventry
Westmorland	Carlisle, Chester
Wiltshire	Salisbury
Worcestershire	Worcester, Hereford
Yorkshire	York, Chester

DIOCESE-COUNTY

Diocese	County
Bath & Wells	Somersetshire
Bristol	Dorset, Bristol
Canterbury	Kent
Carlisle	Cumberland, Westmorland
Chester	Cheshire, Lancashire Cumberland, Westmorland Yorkshire
Chichester	Sussex
Durham	Durham
Ely	Cambridgeshire
Exeter	Cornwall, Devon
Gloucester	Gloucestershire
Hereford	Herefordshire
Lichfield & Coventry	Staffordshire, Warwickshire
Lincoln	Lincolnshire, Leicestershire, Bedfordshire Buckinghamshire, Huntingdonshire, Hertfordshire
London	Essex, Hertfordshire, London, Middlesex
Norwich	Norfolk, Suffolk
Oxford	Oxford
Peterborough	Northamptonshire
Rochester	Kent
Salisbury	Berkshire, Wiltshire
Winchester	Hampshire, Surrey
York	Yorkshire, Nottinghamshire

CHURCH RECORDS: Church of England

	Dates Covered	No. of Rolls
MARRIAGE RECORDS		
Papers		
London Diocese		
Marriage License Allegations	1597–1851	144
Archdeaconry		
Colchester Marriage Bonds and Allegations	1700–1851	8
Essex Marriage Bonds and Allegations	1693–1849	6
Middlesex Marriage Bonds and Allegations	1667–1851	15
Consistory Court, Essex		
Marriage Bonds and Allegations	1665–1817	18
Commissary Court, London		
Marriage Bonds and Allegations	1681–1731	5
Peculiars		
Good Easter Marriage Bonds and Allegations	1750–1808	1
The Sokens (Thorpe, Walton, Kirby) Marriage Bonds and Allegations	1756–1861	1
Writtle with Roxwell Marriage Bonds and Allegations	1700–1847	1
Southwark		
Licenses for Marriages in the Collegiate Church of St. Saviour	1760–1859	1 it.
Tower Hamlets, Stepney		
Marriage Allegations	1703–1719	1 it.
Westminster, Knightsbridge Chapel		
Marriage Allegations	1667–1669	1 it.

	Dates Covered	No. of Rolls
Bedfordshire		
Marriage Allegations	1812–1875	7
Leicestershire		
Marriage Bonds	1710–1891	64
St. Margaret's		
Marriage Bonds	1671–1862	5
Ulceby with Fordington		
Marriages	1651–1748	1 it.
Norwich		
Norfolk		
Caston		
Marriage Register	1539–1640	1 it.
Wellingham		
Marriage Records	1765–1779	1 it.
Oxford		
Archdeaconry of Oxford		
Marriage Bonds	1618–1668	1
Abstracts of Marriage Bonds	1634–1849	1
Peterborough		
Northamptonshire		
Abington		
Marriage Transcripts	1813–1837	1 it.
Salisbury		
Berkshire Peculiars		
Abstracts of Marriage Bonds	1616–1846	1
Winchester		
Isle of Wight		
Godshill		
Marriages	1678–1837	1
Surrey		
Marriage Allegations, Indexed	1763–1866	1
Worcester		
Marriage Bonds and Allegations, Indexed	1553–1957	366

	Dates Covered	No. of Rolls
York		
Lancashire		
Archdeaconry of Richmond		
Marriage Bonds and Affidavits	1746-1799	48
Nottinghamshire		
Bilborough		
Marriage Licenses	1778-1818	1 it.
Tuxford		
Marriage Licenses	1824-1887	1 it.
Yorkshire		
Selby Peculiar		
Marriage Bonds	1604-1776	1
York, now Ripon		
Marriage Bonds and Allegations	1613-1822	9
York, now Southwell		
Nottinghamshire		
Nottingham		
Marriage Allegations	1594-1875	87
Indexes		
Canterbury Province		
Faculty Office		
Calendar of Licences	1632-1955	14
Registry of the Vicar-General		
Indexes to Marriage Allegations	1660-1921	17
Canterbury Peculiars		
Indexes to Marriage Allegations	1660-1859	2
Carlisle		
Index to Marriage License Bonds	1668-1824	2 it.
Lincoln		
Calendar of Marriage Bonds	1574-1846	20
Salisbury		
Archdeaconry of Berkshire		
Berkshire and Oxford Marriage Bonds	1616-1846	2

	Dates Covered	No. of Rolls
Registers		
Canterbury Province		
Register to the Records of the Prerogative Court of Canterbury, all classes		1 it.
Faculty Office		
Register of Marriage Allegations and Calendars of Marriage Licenses	1632–1851 1632–1955	
Registry of the Vicar-General		
Register of Marriage Allegations and Indexes	1660–1851 1660–1921	252
Lichfield and Coventry		
Marriage Licenses, Bonds and Allegations	1636–1880	
Worcester		
Marriage Bonds and Allegations	1660–1957	359
Indexes to the Calendar of Marriage Bonds, and Index Libri Allegationem Matrimonialium	1666–1671	2
PROBATE RECORDS		
Papers[1]		
Canterbury Province		
Prerogative Court	1383–1858	2944
Bristol		
Archdeaconry		
Dorset*	1568–1857	118
Consistory Court		
Deanery of Bristol	1571–1857	75
Dorset Division	1568–1855	33

---

[1]Most entries refer to wills and letters of administration, and those which contain act books or other documents are indicated by an asterisk. Probate before 1858 was under Church of England authority; after 1858, it was a civil function of the Registrar-General.

	Dates Covered	No. of Rolls
Peculiars, Dorset		
Corfe Castle	1576–1846	4
Great Canford and Poole	1650–1857	10
Milton Abbas	1683–1811	1
Sturminster Marshall	1641–1857	3
Wimbourne Minster	1603–1857	8
Woolland	1683–1811	1
Canterbury Diocese		
Archdeaconry		
Canterbury	1449–1858	210
Rochester	1453–1858	155
Consistory Court	1396–1857	117
Peculiars		
Cliff	1671–1845	1
Wingham	1471–1546	1
Carlisle		
Consistory Court	1564–1858	264
Probate Registry		
Ravenstonedale and Temple Sowerby	1690–1850	6
Chester		
Consistory Court		
Cheshire	1547–1858	670
Lancashire	1558–1858	1204
Vicar-General		
Cheshire	1558–1858	61
Lancashire	1521–1800	76
Chichester		
Archdeaconry		
Lewes	1541–1857	88

	Dates Covered	No. of Rolls
Consistory Court	1518–1907	76
Peculiars		
Fishbourne and Rumboldswyke	1578–1857	5
Pagham and Tarring	1520–1858	5
Durham		
Consistory Court	1571–1853	93
Peculiars		
Berwick	1832–1893	2
Dean of Allerton	1666–1845	2
Hexhamshire, Northumberland	1695–1706	2 it.
Probate Registry	1540–1800	7
Ely		
Archdeaconry, Ely	1513–1858	39
Chancellor's Court, Cambridge University	1501–1765	19
Consistory Court	1449–1858	51
Peculiars		
Isleham*	1556–1852	8
Thorney	1556–1858	3
Exeter		
Consistory Court		
Cornwall	1570–1858	138
Peculiars		
Deanery of Cornwall	1605–1857	2
Gloucester		
Consistory Court	1541–1858	53
Hereford		
Consistory Court		
Hereford	1517–1858	241
St. David's	1575–1858	27

	Dates Covered	No. of Rolls
Lichfield and Coventry		
Consistory Court*		
Lichfield and Coventry	1494–1857	1896
St. Asaph	1557–1858	65
Peculiars		
Shropshire		
Bridgnorth	1635–1858	5
Broom Hall	1787–1876	1
Ellesmere	1630–1857	2
Press	16th–17th C.	1 it.
Shrewsbury	1661–1857	1
Wombridge	1787–1854	1
Staffordshire		
Tyrley	1694–1834	1
Warwickshire		
Baddesley Clinton	1675–1850	1 it.
Barston	1675–1850	1 it.
Curdworth	1437–1723	1 it.
Knowle	1675–1850	1 it.
Packwood	1675–1850	1 it.
Temple Balsall	1675–1850	1 it.
Lincoln		
Archdeaconry		
[Bedford], Indexed	1496–1858	77
Buckingham	1483–1858	102
Huntingdon		
Hitchin Division	1585–1857	17
Huntingdon Division	1557–1857	66

	Dates Covered	No. of Rolls
Leicester	1500–1858	218
St. Albans	1415–1857	34
Stow	1530–1834	111
Consistory Court, Indexed	1506–1857	704
Dean and Chapter of Lincoln	1534–1834	24
Peculiars		
Huntingdonshire		
Stow Longa	1661–1857	3
Leicester		
St. Margaret	1580–1858	7
Leicestershire		
Evington	1581–1857	2
Groby	1580–1858	5
Rothley	1575–1857	1 it.
Principal Probate Registry, Bedford		
Leighton Buzzard	1537–1828	2
Norwich		
Archdeaconry		
Sudbury	1544–1857	101
Suffolk	1444–1857	221
Consistory Court	1370–1857	289
Peculiars		
Dean and Chapter, Norwich	1572–1857	10
Deanery of Bocking	1627–1857	7
Isleham and Freckenham		7
Kings Lynn	1584–1597	1

	Dates Covered	No. of Rolls
Oxford		
Archdeaconry		
Buckingham	1801-1857	22
Oxford	1528-1857	65
Consistory Court	1672-1858	18
Peculiars		
Chancellor's Court, Oxford University	1577-1747	3
Oxford Peculiars	1574-1736	10
Peterborough		
Consistory Court, Indexed	1467-1858	374
Peculiars		
Ketten with Rixover	1720-1830	3
Northampton	1668-1844	2
Salisbury		
Archdeaconry		
Berkshire	1480-1857	51
Sarum	1528-1857	127
Peculiars		
Sarum	1560-1857	177
Winchester		
Archdeaconry, Surrey	1534-1857	74
Consistory Court	1502-1857	583
Peculiars		
Archbishop of Canterbury	1614-1821	91
Hampshire[2]	1561-1861	13

---

[2]Individually cataloged under name of peculiar.

	Dates Covered	No. of Rolls
Worcester		
Consistory Court*	1493–1857	616
Dean and Chapter of Worcester*	1441–1788	9
Peculiar, Worcester*	1640–1847	18
York Province		
Prerogative Court of the Archbishop with the Exchequer Court of the Dean*	1396–1858	527
York Diocese		
Archdeaconry		
Nottingham	1506–1857	76
Richmond*	1457–1860	1507
Chancery Court of the Archbishop	1427–1858	28
Dean and Chapter of York	1559–1858	106
York Deaneries	1502–1858	79
Peculiars		
York	1438–1858	63
Dean of York	1530–1857	27
Indexes		
Bristol		
Archdeaconry, Dorset List of Probates	1817–1820	1
Carlisle		
Consistory Court Calendar of Wills and Administrations	1650–1786	182
Chester		
Vicar-General Index of Wills Proved	1545–1620	1
Durham		
Consistory Court Calendar of Wills	1650–1786	2
Index and Abstract of Wills	1540–1590	2

	Dates Covered	No. of Rolls
Probate Registry		
Index of Wills	1540-1800	1
Ely		
Peculiar, Thorney		
Index of Wills	1556-1858	1
Lichfield and Coventry		
Peculiar, Bridgnorth		
Index to Wills	1635-1858	1
Lincoln		
Archdeaconry		
Bedford		
Index to Wills and Administrations	1496-1858	3
Stow		
Index to Wills and Administrations	1530-1834	3
Consistory Court		
Index to Wills and Administrations	1506-1857	7
Dean and Chapter of Lincoln		
Index to Wills and Administrations	1641-1827	1
Peculiars, Leicestershire		
St. Margaret		
Abstract of Wills	1580-1858	1 it.
Groby		
Abstract of Wills	1580-1800	1
Principal Probate Registry, Bedford		
Index to Wills and Administrations	1537-1846	3
Other Indexes		
Doctors Commons		
Index to Wills Proved	1782-1846	1 it.
Hertford		
Abstract of Wills	1601-1652	1 it.
Leicester		
Abstract of Wills	1563-1802	27
Index to Wills and Administrations	1605-1858	3
Rutland		
Index to Wills, Administrations and Inventories	1723-1846	1 it.
Incomplete Wills, Administrations, Bonds, and Inventories	1605-1855	2 it.

	Dates Covered	No. of Rolls
Norwich		
Archdeaconry		
Bocking, Goodeaster, and Writtle		
Calendar of Wills	1617–1691	5
Sudbury		
List of Wills Proved	1840–1844	1
Suffolk		
Calendar of Inventories	1582–1824	1
Consistory Court		
Calendar of Administrations	1609–1699	1
Calendar of Wills	1416–1858	4
Peculiars		
Dean and Chapter of Norwich		
Calendar of Wills	1600–1857	10
Isleham and Freckenham		
Index of Wills	1556–1852	1
Playford		
Will Extract	1444–1800	1
Probate Office, Ipswich		
Abstract of Administrations	1609–1699	1
Peterborough		
Archdeaconry, Northampton		
Index to Administrations	1595	1
Entries of Probate[3]	1663–1685	1
Index to Wills	1608–1723	1 it.
Index to Wills and Administrations	1719–1858	1 it.
Register of Wills	1541–1559	1 it.
Consistory Court		
Register of Wills	1541–1858	90
Peculiar, Liddington		
Abstract of Wills	1580–1821	1
Rochester		
Peculiar, Cliffe		
Index to Wills and Administrations	1671–1845	1

---

[3]Cataloged under Birmingham, District Probate Court.

	Dates Covered	No. of Rolls

Salisbury

Archdeaconry

Berkshire
Index to Probate Records — 1508–1857 — 1
Index to Surnames in Wills — 1480–1857 — 1

Sarum
Calendar of Wills — 1526–1857 — 78

Wiltshire
Calendar of Wills — 1557–1851 — 132

Worcester

Consistory Court
Calendar of Wills — 1661–1858 — 4

Peculiar, Worcester
Index to Wills — 1640–1847 — 18

York

Archdeaconry

/Nottingham/
Probate Act Books — 1705–1858 — 2
Card Index to Wills — 1500–1858 — 3

Richmond
Indexes and Act Books — 1748–1858 — 8

Dean and Chapter of York
Inventories of Wills — to 1700 — 8

York Deaneries
Act Books — 1688–1713 — 1

Peculiars

Southwell Collegiate Church
Register and Abstracts of Wills — 1628–1652 — 1 it.

Swaledale Manor
Register of Wills — 1788–1886 — 1

Registers

Chester

Register of Wills and Administrations for Lancashire in the Cheshire Episcopal Consistory Court — 1846–1858

Register to Calendar of Wills and Administrations from Indexes to the Act Books of the Episcopal Court of the Bishop of Worcester — 1661–1858

	Dates Covered	No. of Rolls
OTHER RECORDS		
Papers		
Bristol		
Archdeaconry, Dorset		
Bonds of Guardians	1688–1802	1
Chester		
Sacramental Certificates	1761–1827	2
Ashton-under-Lyne		
Correspondence	1631–1894	1 it.
Terrier of Glebe Lands	1854	1 it.
Euxton		
Register of Candidates Presented		
for Confirmation	1893–1947	1 it.
Manchester		
Workhouse Creed Register	1881–1914	2
Rochdale		
Day Book	1801–1802	1
Durham		
Dean and Chapter of Durham		
Register Extracts[4]	1625–1816	1
Ely		
Episcopal Registry		
Deposition Books, Indexed	1550–1599	1
Exeter		
Cornwall		
Launcells		
Records of the Bishop of Exeter	1537–1837	1 it.
Portlysean		
Sermons	1885–1909	1
Gloucester		
St. Peter's Abbey		
Cartularies	1393–1538	1
Registers of Writs	1327–1414	1

---

[4]Includes some early entries in Latin, 1259–1334. Some pages are cut.

	Dates Covered	No. of Rolls
Little Washbourne, Overbury, Alstone and Teddington		
Confirmation Registers	1878-1956	1 it.
Lichfield and Coventry		
Diocesan Education Council Minute Book	1834-1837	1 it.
Warwickshire		
Tithe Apportionments	1838-1851	8
Ashow		
Society for the Propogation of the Gospel, Minutes	1853-1886	1
Fenny Compton		
Rector's Correspondence	1734-1844	3
Lincoln		
Hertfordshire		
Ashwell		
Sacrament Record	1859-1890	1
Leavesden		
Creed Register[5]	1870-1891	1
Worcester		
District Probate Court, Birmingham		
Record of Episcopal Visitation In Latin	16th C.	1
York		
Nottinghamshire		
Bilborough		
Sacrament Lists	1730-1783	1 it.
Farnsfield		
List of Church Scholars	1789	1 it.
Kirklington		
Seat Assignments, 27 August	1677	1 it.
Rampton		
Easter Book[6]	1683-1713	1 it.

---

[5] There are creed registers for many parochial and non-parochial units. Most of these are cataloged individually by parish or unit.

[6] Incorrectly cataloged as Ragnall, Nottinghamshire.

CHURCH RECORDS: Nonconformists

	Dates Covered	No. of Rolls
GENERAL RECORDS		
Papers		
Cheshire		
Meeting Places of Nonconformists and Roman Catholics	1689–1853	1 it.
DENOMINATIONAL RECORDS		
Papers		
Baptist		
Dorsetshire		
Chard		
List of Members, 21 December	1783	1 it.
Congregational		
Cheshire		
Mobberley		
Lists of Deeds and Names	1782–1864	1 it.
Inghamite		
Yorkshire		
Rodhill near Grindleston		
Account Book of the Chapel	1758–1823	1 it.
Methodist, New Connexion		
Lancashire		
Manchester		
Conference Registers	1798–1837	1
Presbyterian		
List of Ministers	1717–1731	1 it.
Registers of the Presbyterian Church	1624–1953	47
Lancashire		
Bolton, St. Andrew's Chapel		
Session Minutes	1805–1896	1 it.

	Dates Covered	No. of Rolls
Lancaster, St. Peter's Square		
Minute Book	1828-1832	1 it.
Northumberland		
Bedlington		
Session Book	1844-1912	1
Great and Little Bavington		
Session Book	1754-1801	1 it.
Lowick		
Church Records	1848-1935	1
Middleton		
Extracts of Minutes	1817-1938	1
Morpeth		
Minute Books	1835-1872	1
Newcastle		
Session Book, United Presbyterian Church	1872-1881	1 it.
Warwickshire		
Birmingham		
Miscellaneous Records	1853-1949	1
Roman Catholic		
Staffordshire		
Confirmations	1786-1811	1 it.
Warwickshire		
Ecclesiastical Diary of Bishop Milner, Vicar Apostolic, Middle District, with a few entries by Bishop Walsh	1803-1825 1829-1833	1 it.
Notebook of Mandates of the Bishop of Arras concerning a miracle at Arras	1738	1 it.
Society of Friends (Quakers)		
Buckinghamshire		
Minutes of the Monthly Meeting	1669-1676	1 it.
Cheshire		
Meeting Places of Quakers	1846	1 it.
Devonshire		
Quarterly Meeting Minutes	1653-1729	1 it.
Dorsetshire		
Dorset and Hampshire Quarterly Meeting Records	1661-1729	1 it.

	Dates Covered	No. of Rolls
Durham		
Quarterly Meeting Records	1647–1837	1 it.
Stockton		
Minute Book	1755–1761	1
Nottinghamshire		
Derby and Nottingham Quarterly Meeting Records	1659–1839	1
Warwickshire		
Birmingham		
Records and Minutes	1660–1890	60
Warwick		
Minute Books and Burial Records	1703–1881	5

IV CORPORATE RECORDS

CORPORATE RECORDS: National

	Dates Covered	No. of Rolls
BRITISH EAST INDIA COMPANY		
Papers		
Ecclesiastical Returns (Births, Marriages, and Deaths)		
Bengal, Presidency of		
Church of England Returns, Indexed	1713–1948	526
Roman Catholic Returns, Indexed	1842–1856	6
Bombay, Presidency of		
Church of England Returns, Indexed	1709–1948	164
Roman Catholic Returns, Indexed	1842–1854	5
Burma		
Returns	1937–1950	6
Fort Marlborough		
Returns, Indexed	1759–1825	2 it.
Kerala		
Returns, Indexed	1751–1804	1
Macao		
Returns, Indexed	1820–1833	2 it.
Madras, Presidency of		
Church of England Returns, Indexed	1698–1948	142
Roman Catholic Returns, Pt. Indexed	1777–1884	12
Prince of Wales Island		
Returns	1805–1829	2 it.
Testamentary Records		
Bengal		
Indexed	1710–1937	218
Bombay		
Indexed	1710–1937	28
Madras		
Indexed	1723–1937	144

	Dates Covered	No. of Rolls
Indexes		
Calendar of Probates of English Subjects of District Courts of India, Indexed	1865–1936	23
Registers		
Register to the Collection of Ecclesiastical Returns and Testamentary Records		

CORPORATE RECORDS: Local

	Dates Covered	No. of Rolls
GUILDS		
Papers		
Durham		
Sunderland		
Indigent Sick Society		
Patient Records	1838-1914	1
Lincolnshire		
Barrow Upon Humber		
Clockmakers' Company		
Records	1730	1
Northumberland		
Morpeth		
Butcher, Steiner and Glover Company		
Papers	1719-1805	1 it.
Newcastle		
Guilds and Admissions Book, Indexed	1645-1908	6
Bakers and Brewers Company		
Apprentices and Freemen	1578-1814	
Minutes and Admittances	1753-1910	1
Glovers Company		
Minutes and Apprentice Register	1636-1677	2 it.
Goldsmiths Company		
Extracts	1702-1807	1 it.
Ropers Company		
Extracts	1655-1835	1 it.
Sadlers Company		
Freemens' Bonds	1712-1830	1
Minutes and Apprentices' Register	1509-1707	1 it.
Skinners Company		
Ledger and Register	1696-1878	2 it.
Company of Smiths		
Freemen	1600-1845	1

V PERSONAL RECORDS

The dimensions of this category are voluminous and complex. The material
is subdivided chiefly by the dictates of cataloging, in that some material has a
surname orientation, whereas other material is found by geographic orientation.
There are four sub-classes in this section:

        (1)   Personal Papers – by surname
        (2)   Collections – by name of compiler
        (3)   Pedigrees – by place name
        (4)   Family Histories – by surname

Whenever possible the archive or library where the records were filmed has been
included in the listing. In many instances, the Society has filmed only parts of
the original materials in an archive; yet in some cases, original materials,
dispersed by sale or storage changes over a period of many years, are consolidated in the Society's collection, as filming covered the scattered parts in the
various archives where they are currently deposited.

The Genealogical Society has begun a program to catalog each part of the
collections by locality. Some are more fully cataloged than others. To retrieve
the collections, it is therefore necessary to look under the name of the compiler
in the direct card catalog and under locality in the indirect file. The Society
is converting all of its manuscripts to film. Several of the entries in this
Inventory refer to the original manuscript and will be found listed only in the
direct file under name of compiler. Once the filming is completed, indirect file
cards will also be found.

For some collections, there is a special register or index of contents.
These guides vary in completeness. They describe the kinds of materials included
and may list corresponding call numbers.

In this Inventory, each collection is listed alphabetically by name of
compiler. The archive or library where the collection was microfilmed is given
in parentheses for reference. Again, in most instances the Society has filmed
only parts of the original collection. For some, however, filming of scattered
parts of an original set of manuscripts in several archives has consolidated a
collection.

In addition to the sub-classes already mentioned for this section, the
following table represents individual catalog entries, some of which are multiple
burial ground/parish churchyard entries, from the monumental inscriptions collection which is held by the Society. These entries are individually cataloged by
parish or by churchyard in the indirect file. Printed volumes are included in
the table, also cataloged inscriptions which are printed in local archaeological
and record society journals and printed histories. Although these items are not
yet totally microfilmed, they are included here as items of interest.

County	Printed Lists	Manuscript or Typescript	Record Collections or Scribes
Bedfordshire	4	18	British Mission Collection Gerish Collection Norman Collection
Berkshire	20	26	Payne Collection Sherwood Collection Frederick S. Snell Collection
Buckinghamshire	8	26	Payne Collection Sherwood Collection
Cambridgeshire	3	9	George Minns Collection W. M. Palmer
Cheshire	19	45	F. C. Beazley/J. Paul Rylands John Bennett Collection British Mission Collection Alfred Burton Collection Alan Dale Collection Norman Collection
Cornwall	1	15	F. Wall List
Cumberland	9	7	Edwin Dodds with J. W. Robinson
Derbyshire	9	24	G. Allen British Mission Collection Norman Collection
Devonshire	5	10	
Dorsetshire	1	6	British Mission Collection Vernal G. Wardell
Durham	4	13	British Mission Collection Herbert M. Wood
Essex	32	6	James Harvey Bloom Collection J. J. Howard & H. Farnham Burke Norman Collection

County	Printed Lists	Manuscript or Typescript	Record Collections or Scribes
Gloucestershire	64	18	James Harvey Bloom Collection British Mission Collection Percy Charles Rushen Edith Mary Woodford
Hampshire	6	22	British Mission Collection
Herefordshire	9	3	Gerish Collection Hertfordshire Collection
Hertfordshire	4	147	British Mission Gerish Collection R. B. Payne Collection
Huntingtonshire	0	2	W. M. Wilmott
Kent	72	31	British Mission Collection G. E. Cokayne L. L. Duncan Thomas C. Ferguson David E. Gardner Victor L. Palmer Thomas Shindler (1892) Rev. Christopher Hales Wilkie (1893)
Lancashire	19	243	F. C. Beazley James Bibby Collection British Mission Collection Burnley Central Library Collection William Farrer Collection David E. Gardner Clifford Hartley Lancashire Collection E. Bodin Leech, W. Ed. White Norman Collection Owen Collection
Leicestershire	3	163	British Mission Collection Evelyn Gent Thomas John Grewcock Mr. Hartop, E. Morris Ada L. Lenton
Lincolnshire	2	31	British Mission Collection
Monmouthshire	3	9	British Mission Collection

County	Printed Lists	Manuscript or Typescript	Record Collections or Scribes
Norfolk	28	115	British Mission Collection Clifford Hartley G. H. Holley Norfolk Collection J. Beach Whitmore Collection
Northamptonshire	8	4	William A. Caffall
Northumberland	31	32	Thomas Bell Collection G. E. Cokayne Rev. John Hodgson Norman Collection Society of Antiquaries Manuscript Collection
Nottinghamshire	9	33	British Mission Collection Margaret Jill Higton, Derek A. Cuthbert
Oxfordshire	7	3	Frederick S. Snell Collection
Rutlandshire	1	2	
Somersetshire	20	24	British Mission Collection Sherwood Collection
Shropshire	14	4	
Staffordshire	50	16	British Mission Collection G. E. Cokayne David E. Gardner Staffordshire Collection
Suffolk	53	27	British Mission Collection
Surrey	30	34	George S. Allen, copied from Rev. Kerry C. M. N. Booker Alfred Ridley Box British Mission Collection George Edward Cokayne A. M. Colliard Edith Mary Woodford

County	Printed Lists	Manuscript or Typescript	Record Collections or Scribes
Sussex	29	45	British Mission Collection Edward H. W. Dunkin Collection J. Beach Whitmore
Warwickshire	9	20	Edward G. Armstrong James Harvey Bloom Collection British Mission Collection
Westmorland	1		
Wiltshire	34	14	Vernal G. Wardell
Worcestershire	12	9	David E. Gardner, James Harvey Bloom Collection
Yorkshire	30	220	British Mission Collection Sidney Cramer Arthur Jackson (1895) Norman Collection A. T. Rollinson Sherwood Collection Frank Smith Ralph Thoresby Collection Yorkshire Collection

PERSONAL RECORDS: Personal Papers

	Dates Covered	No. of Rolls
Butler, James, Duke of Ormonde Letter from Charles II, King of Great Britain, enclosing oath of allegiance (Fairfax Collection)	1658	1 it.
Ewen, Alfred (fl. 1921) Diary of Visits to Parishioners. "The first 50 pages parish property, the rest is mine . . . better than wasting so fine a book . . ."	1921	1 it.
Hare, Thomas Abstracts of Title to an Estate in Fincham, Norfolk, 1 vol. manuscript	1756-1816	
Jenkins, Sir Leoline Directions for Conducting his Funeral, 12 June (National Library of Wales)	1685	1 it.
Morgan, John Indenture between John Morgan of St. Giles in the Fields and John Bradley of York	1706	1 it.
Park, Henry The Surgeon and his Register. Copied by F. C. Beazley		1 it.
Percy, Algernon Family Record of the Duke of Northumberland (Newcastle Public Library)		1 it.
Sanderson, Christopher Diary and Pedigree. Eggleston, Durham. Copied by F. C. Beazley, 19 pp manuscript	1905	
Spilsbury, Thomas Abstracts of Title to Farm Called "Linch" in Little Hereford, Hereford, 1 vol. manuscript	1709-1778	
Verney, John Peyton, Lord Willoughby de Broke (1738-1816) Northamptonshire and Leicestershire Accounts (Society of Genealogists)	1798	1 it.
Warrenne, John de, Earl of Warrenne and Surrey (1286-1347) A Collection of Loose Papers, including letters and newspaper clippings. (Doncaster Central Library)		3
Young, Sir William Lawrence Letters and Papers of Sir William Lawrence Young and his Family. Copied by George Frederick T. Sherwood, 1 vol. manuscript	1641-1853	

PERSONAL RECORDS: Manuscript Collections

	Dates Covered	No. of Rolls
Manuscript Collections for a History of Sunderland, Durham, c. 1932. Includes a street by street description with chronological accounts of each property transaction, extracts of documents, interviews with local residents and a list of shipbuilders on the Wear River in the 18th and 19th centuries		14
Transcripts of Marriage Bonds, Pedigrees, Parish Registers and other Documents. (Written by the same author) (Sunderland Public Library)		3
Banks, Charles Edward (fl 1923) Genealogical Collections. Includes parish register transcripts, subsidy rolls, genealogical notes on Cleeve, Pepperall, Gardiner, Morton families. Table of contents at beginning of film. (Library of Congress, Special Collections)	c.1523-1653	4
Bartelot, Richard Grosvenor Historical Notes on Devon, Dorset (Society of Genealogists, Genealogical Society of Utah). Includes index of court rolls, pedigrees, parish register transcripts, marriages.	1561-1812	6 it.
Beazley, F. C. Collectanea for Lancashire and Cheshire. Includes monumental inscriptions, local pedigrees, genealogical notes. (Society of Genealogists)		13
Beckwith, Thomas (18th c.) Genealogical and Historical Manuscripts Pertaining to Yorkshire, Durham, and Northumberland. Includes pedigrees, collections of arms, crests, lists of deaths (18th c.), monumental inscriptions, memoranda, extracts from Domesday. (Yorkshire Archaeological Society, Historical Society of Pennsylvania)	c.1066-1800	15 it., 1
Bell, Thomas Collections. Includes monumental inscriptions, company papers, parish records, lists of names (doctors, lawyers, school children, sailmakers), militia returns, ratebooks. (Society of Antiquaries, Newcastle Upon Tyne)	c.1785-1825	4

	Dates Covered	No. of Rolls
Bennett, John Genealogical and Historical Materials of Cheshire. Includes pedigrees, genealogies, topography, parish registers, probate records, marriages, monumental inscriptions, newsclippings, and a list of British inns and hotels of Chester, 1840, with descriptions. Table of contents on first roll of film. (Cheshire Record Office)	c.1200-1945	14
Bernau, Charles Allan See London.		
Betton, Charles Steuart Genealogical Collections Relating to Shropshire Families. Includes scrap pedigrees of the bishops of Hereford. (Shrewsbury Public Library)		8
Bibby, James Collections, Lancashire. Includes parish register transcripts, monumental inscriptions, newsclippings, miscellaneous family records (with surname index), Baron family burials, will extracts. Nobel, Calvert, Cuncliffe, Dowbiggin, Shaw, Pilling, Bond, Baron families. (Genealogical Society of Utah)		12, 43 it.
Bickley, William B. Pedigrees and Genealogical Papers. Includes transcripts of parish registers, wills, pedigrees, and other records. Indexed	1700-1928	8
Manuscript Notes and Materials relating to the History of Yardley. (Birmingham Reference Library)		1 it.
Bloom, James Harvey (b. 1860) Manuscript Collections for Warwickshire, Gloucestershire, Worcestershire. Includes notes on local topography, parish register extracts, monumental inscriptions, wills, deeds, court records. Index first 4 rolls of film. (Shakespeare Library, Society of Genealogists)		23
Yorkshire Manuscripts (Society of Genealogists)		1
Genealogical Notes for Herefordshire Arranged by parish. (Society of Genealogists)		1 it.
Boyd, Sir Percival Original Workbook for the compilation of "Boyd's Marriages."[1] (Genealogical Society of Utah), 1 vol. manuscript.		

---

[1]Refer to Boyd's Marriage Index (174 rolls) in RESEARCH AIDS, Church Records.

	Dates Covered	No. of Rolls

Brandwood Manuscripts
    Historical Data on Towns of Salford Hundred,
    Lancashire. Copied by B.W.T. Norman, 1
    vol. manuscript

Burrell, Herbert
    Genealogical and Family History Collections,
    Norfolk and Suffolk Families. Includes news-
    paper clippings from local papers, photographs,
    typewritten histories of the Burrell, Cogman,
    and Read families, and pedigree charts.   3
    (Genealogical Society of Utah)   5 it.

Buxton Manuscripts
    Collections for Norfolk. (Society of Genealogists)   1 it.

Challen, William Harold
    Transcripts of Parish Registers and Bishops' Tran-
    scripts. Cataloged individually by parish.
    (Guildhall Library)   50

    Register of Call Numbers for the Challen Collection,   50
    1 vol. manuscript

Chaloner, Thomas (fl. 1592)
    Sundry Notes and Genealogies. Includes pedigrees,   14th-
    descents   15th C.   1 it.

    Thomas Chaloner's Booke of Chester Bridgestreet,
    Student of the lawe of armes and armory. A
    Booke of sundrye and divers noats of evidences
    of tymes and witnesses of Cheshire, Lancashire
    and Wales.[2] (National Library of Wales)   1592   1

Clark, Wyndham D.
    Pedigrees and Genealogical Information relating
    to Welsh, Scots, and English Families. (National
    Library of Wales)   2

Clay, John William
    Yorkshire Collections. Includes the materials
    collected for Clay's edition of Dugdale's
    Visitation of Yorkshire   10

    Collectanea Genealogiarum . . . Nobilium et
    Generosorum . . . . Includes abstracts of wills,
    transcripts of parish registers and miscellaneous
    papers, collected for his "Extinct and Dormant
    Peerages" of the Northern Counties.   1 it.

    Collection of Notes and Abstracts relating to the
    Benson Family   1

    Collections of Lincolnshire Families   6

---

[2]Part of the Norman Yoke controversy of the 16th century.

	Dates Covered	No. of Rolls

Collections and Notes on many Yorkshire Families. Each of these are individually cataloged in the direct file under Clay. (Yorkshire Archaeological Society)   — 11 it., 2

Clayton, Edward (1779-1865)
Manuscript Collections for a History of Fairfield, Derbyshire. Includes index of inhabited houses with description and history of each house and family.   — 2

Cope, Gilbert
Collection of Family Data on American Families with British Origins /Quaker families 7, Indexed. (Genealogical Society of Pennsylvania)   — 75

Collection of English and Irish Notes. (Genealogical Society of Pennsylvania)   — 1 it.

Coulthard Manuscripts
Genealogical Case Files. Includes parish register transcripts for various families, pedigrees, research slips, census extracts and correspondence with clients. Indexed. (Carlisle Castle)   — 4

Crofton, Henry Thomas (fl. 1900)
Genealogical Data on Cheshire and Lancashire Families. (Manchester Public Library)   — 6

Dale, Alan
Records of Local Cheshire Persons. Includes will extracts, clubs, church registers, family bibles, pedigrees, miscellaneous titles, and tax assessments. Arranged alphabetically by name. (Worcestershire Record Office)   — 5

Manuscript Collections for a History of Cheshire. Scrapbooks and record extracts from census, undertakers' funeral registers, chapel and burial ground plans, especially Nonconformists records.   — 2 it.

Davies, Isaac (fl. 1900)
Collections for a History of Birkenhead, Cheshire. Historical scrapbook of newsclippings, record extracts, letters. In Welsh. (National Library of Wales)   — 1 it.

Drew Manuscripts
Collections for a History of Sussex. Includes index to Sussex wills, interspersed with pedigrees. (Sussex Record Office)   1406-1730 1

	Dates Covered	No. of Rolls

Dugard Manuscripts
Collections for Norfolk. Includes parish register transcripts and newspaper clippings on local historians and their collections, pedigree cases in law courts, and announcements of the sale of historical manuscripts. (Norfolk Archaeological Society)   1

Dunkin, Edward, H. W.
Historical Collections for Sussex. Working notebooks, vols. 100-136 only. (Sussex Record Office)   6

Farnham, George Francis
Medieval Village Notes of Leicestershire. (Leicester City Museum)   2

Farrer, William (fl. 1900)
Collections for Lancashire, Yorkshire. Includes pedigrees, genealogies, evidences, military records, taxes, coats of arms, tenures, rent rolls. Christopher Townley mannuscripts, Phillips manuscripts. (Manchester Public Library)   19

Fletcher, W. G. D.
Collections for /a History of/ Shropshire, Staffordshire and Leicestershire. Includes transcripts of parish registers, genealogies, and other documents   11

Glencross, Reginald M.
Manuscript Collections for Cornwall. Includes parish register transcripts, extracts of wills from the Prerogative Court of Canterbury. Cataloged separately, 24 vol. manuscript

Hall, W. T.
Historical Collections of Dadlington, Leicestershire. Includes transcripts of parish registers, a description of the parish with extracts from poll taxes, censuses, and other records. (Society of Genealogists)   1

Hayhurst, T. H.
Collections for Lancashire. Includes miscellaneous records and lecture notes on Old Radcliffe. (Genealogical Society of Utah)   2

Henderson, Charles J. (fl. 1920)
Collections for a History of Cornwall. Includes pedigrees, lay subsidies, deeds, freeholder's lists, parish register transcripts, notes of the Trwinnard and Nepean families, notes for several parishes, calendars of Cornish manuscripts (37 vols. of 65 filmed), Cornish manuscripts at Nettlecomb Court, Somerset. Part indexed. (County Museum of Cornwall)   24

Description List of the Henderson Collection   1 it.

	Dates Covered	No. of Rolls
Hodgson, Rev. John Manuscript Collections for a History of Northumberland. Includes pedigrees of Northumberland families. (Newcastle-Upon-Tyne Public Library)		7
Ince, Thomas Norris See entry for John Sykes		
Kendall, H. P. Manuscript Collections for Yorkshire.[3] Includes copies of the manuscripts of Edward Johnson Walker, the Halifax Historian (manuscript 627), and epitaphs in the Halifax churchyard. (Yorkshire Archaelogical Society)		1 it.
Laycock, J. A. Transcripts of Parish Registers for Lancashire Parishes. With family notes, wills, pedigrees. (Burnley Central Library)		8
Leighton, Henry Reginald Genealogy Notes for Durham, Northumberland. (Society of Genealogists)		2 it.
Lloyd, Howard Williams Manuscripts relating to Pennsylvania, England, and Wales. (National Library of Wales)		1 it.
Longden, Henry Isham (fl. 1925) Manuscript Collection. Includes parish register extracts with other notes and lists, wills, and administrations. Indexed. (Northampton Record Office)		19
Marley, T. W. Genealogical Collections for Northumberland. Includes his notebooks #170-175 and extracts of Halmote records. (Society of Antiquaries, Newcastle Upon Tyne)		4
Minns, George Manuscript Collections. Includes parish register transcripts, extracts from court records, monumental inscriptions, transcripts of wills, and other records.	1558-1889	11
Genealogical Gleanings		1 it.

---

[3]The card catalog identifies several manuscripts as compiled by Kendall. The manuscript catalog of the Yorkshire Archaelogical Society where the materials were filmed lists these same materials under local records without authorship.

	Dates Covered	No. of Rolls

Manuscript Collections for a History of Soham, Cambridgeshire. Includes parish register transcripts, obituaries, newspaper clippings, articles, notes, 3 vols. manuscript

Extracts and Notes on Many Families. These are individually cataloged in the direct file under George Minns. There is no separate register, and the majority of them are original manuscripts, 24 vols. manuscript

Morris, George
    Genealogical Manuscript of Shropshire, Indexed. (Shrewsbury Public Library)   6

Mount, Ira William
    Historical and Genealogical Collections for Berkinghamshire. Includes miscellaneous records for St. Albans, 1 vol. manuscript

    Transcripts of Church Registers, Marriages, Non-parochial Registers, and Other Records   4 it.

Norman, Bertram William Tuff
    Manuscript Collections for Lancashire, arranged alphabetically. Includes numerous parish register transcripts, monumental inscriptions, copies of documents and record collections, manuscript histories and collections of pedigrees, newspaper clippings. Each item is individually cataloged, some under locality, some under Norman, some under subject. There is no master list or index, the total number of manuscripts is unknown. (Genealogical Society of Utah)   1500–1850   1

Owen, John (b. 1815)
    Manuscript Collections, Lancashire. Includes monumental inscriptions, parish registers, genealogical memoranda, architectural and archaeological notes, and miscellaneous historical notes for Manchester and the surrounding area. (Manchester Free Reference Library)   34

    Index to the Owen Manuscripts in the Manchester Free Public Library. Compiled by Ernest Axon, 1900, as Occasional List #6 and typed by the Genealogical Society of Utah, 1959, 1 vol. manuscript

Paver, William (fl. 1834)
    Manuscript Collections. Includes pedigrees of Yorkshire families, 600 pedigrees from visitations, arranged alphabetically, and genealogies of Yorkshire families from various sources.   1530,1584
    Indexed   1612   5 it.

	Dates Covered	No. of Rolls
Nomina Villarum for Yorkshire, 9 Edw II. Different from Harleian Manuscript 6281 with additional entries for the Wapentake of Holderness and wills outside of that Wapentake. Copy made by "J.W."		1 it.
Phipps, H. R. Manuscript Collections for Somerset. Includes abstracts of court records, deeds and jurors' lists		3 it.
Pilley, Walter Collections for Herefordshire. Includes pedigrees from visitations, correspondence between Pilley and George W. Marshall describing Harleian Manuscripts and Visitations compiled for George Carpenter (b. 1667), and other record extracts. (Hereford Public Library)	1896	2 it.
Prattinton, Peter Manuscript Collections for a History of Worcester- shire, vols. 1-46. Pt. Indexed. (Society of Antiquaries)		14
Radcliffe, William Manuscript Collections, Lancashire, Yorkshire. Includes military and court records, pedigrees, personal documents, letters and memoranda, marriages, and Dugdale's Yorkshire Visitations.	1665-1666	6
Papers relating mostly to marriage registers and legislation respecting marriages	1753	1 it.
Sundry pedigrees with rough notes and a list of Yorkshire peculiars. (Yorkshire Archaeological Society)		1
Richardson, Moses A. Collection Genealogica: The Family History of the North of England. Includes extracts from guild records, poll books, church registers, and a prospectus for History of the Antient Towns of Newcastle and Gateshead. (Society of Antiquaries, Newcastle Upon Tyne)		1
Roe, Eric Arthur Genealogical Collections, Gloucestershire, Suffolk, Wiltshire, and Somersetshire. Includes pedigrees, extracts of wills, parish registers on the ances- tors of Eric Roe. (Genealogical Society of Utah)	c.1600-1950	9
Rusby, James Historical Documents Relating to Yorkshire. Indexed	17th- 19th C.	1

	Dates Covered	No. of Rolls

Shaw, Giles (fl. 1885)
      Manuscript Collections for Lancashire. Includes
      Oldham parish register transcripts, clippings,
      and miscellaneous data. Table of contents, 1st
      roll. (Manchester Public Library)   19

Sherwood, George Frederick T. (fl. 1900)
      Manuscript Collections   349+

           The Sherwood Collection requires more than a
      summary entry because of its size and its unique
      contents. It includes several original manu-
      scripts in addition to the rolls of microfilm.
      Listing these manuscripts is difficult since all
      of them are individually cataloged, some under
      locality, some under Sherwood, and some under
      subject. No complete master list of the original
      exists, but a complete cross-referenced, three-way
      index to the collection is being compiled

      The collection is organized in these sections:

      Research Case Files.

      Sherwood was a professional genealogist and his
      case files include photographs, correspondence,
      original documents, referrals from American genea-
      logists, ads, and publicity he received for his
      work. These files are divided into current research
      files, research by families, and research by locali-
      ties. Sherwood duplicated every document for each
      name and locality included. The Register of Contents,
      prepared by the Genealogical Society Cataloging
      Department, describes the general contents of these
      files and gives corresponding call number

      Research Finding Aids and Indexes.

      Sherwood compiled these to speed access to his own
      collection and to original sources in archives and
      libraries which he used. Some of these are described
      in the Register of Contents, some are individually
      cataloged. These are representative:

	Dates Covered	No. of Rolls
Indexes to Court Records		1 it.
Chancery Proceedings	1790	
Close Rolls, 1700	1700	
Close Rolls from Enrollments	1700-1750	
Dramatis Personae: Names and Places Appearing in Selective Documents from Various English Court Records, 1 vol. manuscript		
Lancashire and Cheshire Cooperative Search, Index to Surnames		1 it.

	Dates Covered	No. of Rolls
List of 6000 Berkshire Wills, PCC, with references to 622 pedigrees, 1 vol. manuscript	1631-1745	
Parentalia from the Public Record Office, 2 vols. manuscripts--		
Exchequer Depositions	1760-1840	
War Office Returns of Officer's Service	1828	
Durham Registrar's Bills and Answers	1618-1695	
King's Bench, Articles of Clerkship	1749-1785	
Sherwood Indexes to Genealogical Data in the Records of Lawsuits, Wills, Parish Registers, Pedigrees, 5 vols. manuscripts		
Extracts from the Consistory Court of Richmond, and the Peculiar Court of Masham	1819-1824 1820-1823	1 it.

Sherwood wrote on the recto (right-hand) page
first and the verso (left-hand) page back
through the book in all of his bound volumes.
And they must be read that way to make sense

The Sherwood Slip Index.

Sherwood compiled his own research index to
persons and subjects in important record
categories. This index is _not_ an index to his
case files nor to his finding aids, although
some entries may be found there. The index
contains 2 million 2" x 1" slips. The following analysis of the Slip Index was made by
Dr. Louis Marks, Dean of Biology, St. Joseph's
College, Philadelphia

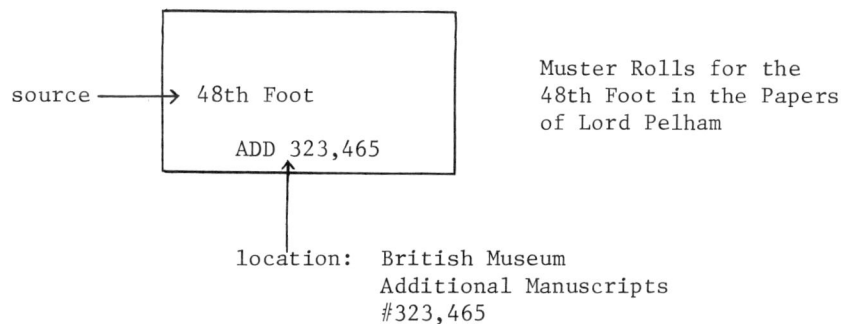

source ———→ 48th Foot

ADD 323,465

Muster Rolls for the
48th Foot in the Papers
of Lord Pelham

location: British Museum
Additional Manuscripts
#323,465

	Dates Covered	No. of Rolls

The index also includes these records:

  27,000 unclaimed dividends in the Bank of
       England
146,000 baptisms, marriages and burials not
       yet printed
115,000 Exchequer depositions
  34,863 extracts from the Court of Requests
  26,272 extracts from Star Chamber Proceedings

A complete index to 212 volumes of Notes and
Queries, 1849-1950; peerage cases; local history
journals; Betham letters; Chancery proceedings
(1386 is earliest); imprinted Curia Regis Rolls
(1196-1237); PCC wills; British Army regiments
and their histories; with a complete list of
muster rolls and an analysis of every battle in
which the British have fought

Snell, Frederick Simon
    Collection of Sources pertinent to Genealogical
    Research for Berkshire and Oxfordshire. Includes
    extracts of wills and administrations, chancery
    depositions, monumental inscriptions. General
    Index. (Society of Genealogists)

	1559-1737	27

Steele, Frederick M.
    Families of England and America Collection.
    Includes photographs, newspaper clippings,
    ancestral sketches. (Genealogical Society of
    Pennsylvania)

		5

Sykes, John
    Sykes and Ince's Genealogical Collections of
    Yorkshire. Includes parish registers, wills,
    deeds, and other genealogical records. Also
    the correspondence between Sykes and Ince and
    their clients. (Doncaster Central Library)

		39

Sykes, W.
    History and Genealogy of Yorkshire Families.
    Includes newspaper clippings. Pt. Indexed.
    (Leeds Public Library)

		15

Thoresby, Ralph (1658-1725)
    Manuscript Collections. Includes 1704 Window
    tax for West Riding of Yorkshire, gazeteer
    (visitation roster), subscriptions of Ms
    Ducatus Leodiensis, epitaphs, diary of
    Thoresby's journey to Northern England and
    Scotland, epitaphs of London copied.
    (Yorkshire Archaeological Society)

	1677 1712,1714	1 it.

Tomkin, Thomas
    Materials for the History of Ancient Cornwall
    with Pedigrees of the Early Landowners.
    (County Museum of Cornwall)   1

Whitmore, Major John Beach (fl. 1940)
    Historical and Genealogical Collections. Includes
    church notes for Hampshire and Oxfordshire, and
    monumental inscriptions for Norfolk, Sussex, and   2
    London. (Society of Genealogists)   5 it.

PERSONAL RECORDS: Pedigrees

	Dates Covered	No. of Rolls
PEDIGREES BY NATION		
Fairfax, Lady, of Cameron Heraldry Manuscripts of England		1 it.

[Heane, William C.]
    [Pedigrees] copies from Harleian Manuscripts
    in the British [Museum]
		1

Keith, Charles Penrose
    Manuscript Pedigrees with Alphabetical Name List.
    (Genealogical Society of Pennsylvania)
		2

Norman, Bertram William Tuff English Pedigrees		2
Norman Collection Pedigrees. (Genealogical Society of Utah)		1 it.

Paget, Gerald
    Genealogies of European Families from Charlemagne
    to the present, 1957. Alphabetical. (Genealogical
    Society of Utah)
		5

Phillips, Sir Thomas
    Pedigrees from various counties of England and
    Wales. (Cardiff Central Library)
		1 it.

Miscellaneous Collections of Pedigrees, Genealogical
    Notes, Coats of Arms and Descents for England
    and Wales. (Cardiff Central Library, Genealogical
    Society of Utah)
	16th-
	19th C.
		19 it.

PEDIGREES BY COUNTY		
<u>Berkshire</u>		
Norman, B. W. T. Coats of Arms in Berkshire Churches.		1
<u>Cambridgeshire</u>		

Phillipps, Sir Thomas
        Visitation of Cambridgeshire and Cornwall
        Arms. Phillipps manuscript 8799. (County
        Museum of Cornwall)
		1

	Dates Covered	No. of Rolls

Cheshire

Beazley, F. C.
 Lancashire and Cheshire Pedigrees. (Society
 of Genealogists) — 1 it.

Dugdale, Sir William
 Visitation of Wirral Hundred, Cheshire.
 Transcripts of pedigrees from the College
 of Arms copy by John P. Rylands. Indexed.
 (Society of Genealogists) — 1663-1664 — 2 it.

Eedes, J.
 Cheshire Pedigrees from Visitation of — 1566
 Cheshire. Harleian Manuscripts. Notes — 1424,1505
 in blue ink from "The Visitation of William
 Flower, also Robert Glover, Somerset
 Herald then his Marshall for ye county of
 Chester, AD 1580 . . ." with some additions
 from the Rawlinson Manuscripts and from
 manuscripts at Eaton Hall, Cheshire, 1 vol.
 manuscript

Massie, Rev. Richard (fl. 1806)
 Genealogies. Transcribed from a manuscript — 1566-1580,
 including visitation of Cheshire by William — 1613
 Flower, 1566, Robert Glover, 1580, and Richard
 St. George, 1613. Copy of same manuscript in
 possession of John Clegg of Neston, Esq.
 (d. 1804), 1 vol. manuscript

Norman, B. W. T.
 Cheshire Pedigrees. Copies from Harleian — 1613
 Manuscript and College of Arms Manuscript C6. — 1535,1070
 (Society of Genealogists) — 1

 Arms of Cheshire Families. Note on first
 page, "Given by Col. T. Brown to T. T.
 Windsor, June, 1810." 1 vol. manuscript — 1810

 Facsimiles of Genealogies, Wills, Pedigrees,
 and Arms relating to Cheshire Families, 1
 vol. manuscript

 Pedigrees of Northwich — 1 it.

Cornwall

Arms of the Gentry of Cornwall. Compiled, 1959 — 1 it.

Heraldic Church Notes. (County Museum of
 Cornwall) — c.1560-1880 — 1

Notes on Cornish Families — 1

	Dates Covered	No. of Rolls

Phillipps, Sir Thomas
    Visitation of Cambridgeshire and Cornwall
    Arms. Phillipps Manuscript 8799. (County
    Museum of Cornwall)
		1

Rogers, Reginald Cornwall Pedigrees in Book Form. (Genealogical Society of Utah)		5
Sperling, J. H. Heraldic Collections of Cornwall. Includes entries from monuments, pedigrees, "county histories and other reliable sources." Pt. Indexed. (County Museum of Cornwall)		3

Cumberland

Cumberland Visitations by Families. Indexed.		3 it.
Notes on Forty Cumberland Families from Various Wills and Parish Registers.		1 it.
Pedigrees of Cumberland Families with Miscellaneous Notes. Alphabetical by surname		2

Durham

Manuscript Notes on Families of Northumberland and Durham		8
Beckwith, Thomas Pedigrees of the Gentry and Bishoprick of Durham and Northumberland. (Genealogical Society of Utah), 1 vol. manuscript		

Hampshire

Yeoman Families of Greywell Manor		1 it.
Heraldic Visitations of Hampshire	1575,1622, 1686	1 it.

Hertfordshire

Pedigrees and Arms of Hertfordshire Families. Copied from manuscripts in the Heralds' College Museum. Signed J. M. A., 1 vol. manuscript		

Kent

Kentish Pedigrees		1

	Dates Covered	No. of Rolls

Lancashire

Beazley, F. C.
    Lancashire and Cheshire Pedigrees. (Society
      of Genealogists) — 1 it.

Pedigrees of Lancashire and Yorkshire Families — 1

A Selection of Genealogies and Pedigrees in the
    Rochdale Reference Library — 1

Norfolk

Harvey, William
    Visitation of Norfolk. Copied by M. C. I. — 1567
      Betham, Cork Herald, 1 vol. manuscript

Holley, G. H.
    Extracts for Proof of Sir Edward Busshe's
    Visitation of Norfolk. Includes parish
    registers, wills, monumental inscriptions,
    court records, marriage licenses, freemen
    lists, inquisitions post-mortem, Inns of
    Court registers, alumni Cantabrigiensis,
    Oxoniensis, Athenae. Alphabetical.
    (Halesworth, Suffolk) — 1664 — 23

Notes citing the errors and omissions in Busshe's
    "Visitation of Norfolk, 1664." Unindexed,
    manuscript — 1664

Pedigrees compiled from parish registers, wills
    of Norfolk County, 7 vols. manuscript

Miscellaneous Pedigrees and Manuscripts of
    Norfolk Families — 1 it.

Northumberland

Pedigrees of Families of Holy Island, with
    Miscellaneous Documents — 1 it.

Pedigrees of Northumberland Families — 7

Manuscript Notes on Families of Northumberland
    and Durham — 8

Nottinghamshire

Phillimore, W. P. W.
    County Pedigrees for London and Nottingham.
      (Genealogical Society of Utah) — 1 it.

	Dates Covered	No. of Rolls

Shropshire

Hardwick, William
    Pedigrees of the Heralds' Visitations of
    Shropshire. Indexed. (Shrewsbury Public
    Library) 2

Morris, Joseph (fl. 1831)
    Genealogy Manuscripts of Shropshire
    Families. (Shrewsbury Public Library) 5

Newling, Rev. J.
    Pedigrees of Shropshire Families. Includes
    extracts from the Phillipps Manuscripts.
    Indexed. (Shrewsbury Public Library) 2

Shropshire Pedigrees. .... to 18th C.   1 it.

Whitmore, Major John Beach (fl. 1940)
    Shropshire Pedigrees transcribed from
    the Gough Manuscripts. (Society of
    Genealogists) .... 1 it.

Suffolk

Candler, Matthias
    Pedigrees of Suffolk and Essex, 2 vols.
    manuscript. (Genealogical Society of
    Utah)

Fenns Manuscripts
    Pedigrees of Suffolk and Norfolk. Indexed,
    1 vol. manuscript. (Genealogical Society
    of Utah)

Surrey

Heraldic Visitations 1

Pedigrees of Mitcham 1

Sperling, J. H.
    A Collection of Arms on Monuments and
    Paintings in Churches of Surrey. Indexed.
    (Minet Library, Lambeth) .... 1 it.

Sussex

Some Attree Pedigrees. Indexed 6

Wagner, Henry
    Collection of Huguenot Pedigrees in England.
    Alphabetical. (Sussex French Hospital,
    Horsham) 6

	Dates Covered	No. of Rolls

Yorkshire

Bonold, Thomas
    Visitation Pedigrees of Lancashire and
      Yorkshire. Copied by William Reeves.
      (Trinity College Library)
          1531,1580   1

Dade, William
    Pedigrees of Yorkshire Families.
      (Yorkshire Archaeological Society)
          1780   1

Dugdale, William
    Yorkshire Visitation of 1664, Supplement
      to those Omitted in Visitation 1665-1666,
      with continuations and additions to 1827 by
      William Radcliffe. Indexed. (Yorkshire
      Archaeological Society)
          1664-1827   1 it.

Nalson, Robert
    Pedigrees of the Gentry of the West Riding
      of Yorkshire. Transcribed from a manuscript
      in York Minster written by Nalson. (York-
      shire Archaeological Society)
          1674   1 it.

Pedigrees of Lancashire and Yorkshire Families   1

Rusby, James (fl. 1892)
    Pedigrees and Arms of Leeds Families.
      Indexed   1

Yorkshire Pedigrees, temp. Elizabeth I   1 it.

PEDIGREES BY FAMILY

Bradley

The Pedigree Book of the Families of Bradley and
    Honey of Yorkshire and other English Counties   to 19th C.   1 it.

Chalie

Wagner, Henry
    Pedigrees and Account of the Chalie Family.
      (The Hague)   1 it.

Dencher

Pedigrees and Notes on Greystoke, Dencher,
    Hedley, Mather Families. Includes miscellaneous
      pedigrees, A-Z   1

Eure

Pedigree of the Right Honorable Ralph, Lord Eure,
    Baron of Maulton   1 it.

	Dates Covered	No. of Rolls
Greystoke		
See Dencher		
Godolphin		
Notebook Pedigree of the Wynne Family of North Wales and the Godolphin Family of Cornwall		2 it.
Gower		
Pedigree of the Gower Family of the British Isles		1 it.
Griffiths		
Pedigree of the Griffiths of Salop	to 17th C.	1 it.
Pedigree Descent and Arms of Anne, daughter of Walter Gryffin	to 16th C.	1 it.
Hedley		
See Dencher		
Helsby		
Helsby Pedigree of Chestre		1 it.
Herbert		
Pedigree of William Herbert, Earl of Pembroke		1 it.
Honey		
See Bradley		
Ingram		
Pedigrees of the Imgrams of Worcester.[4] (Leeds Central Library)	1700–1800	4
Knollys		
Miscellaneous English and Welsh Pedigrees including the Pedigree of Sir Francis Knollys		2 it.
Longford		
Pedigree of the Longford Family of Shropshire		1 it.
Mather		
See Dencher		

---

[4] Also cataloged under Yorkshire, Leeds, Templenewsam Collection.

	Dates Covered	No. of Rolls
Morris		
Pedigree of Sir J. A. Morris	to 19th C.	1 it.
Rimmington		
Rimmington, W. H. Pedigree of the Rimmington Family		1 it.
Sandwith		
Pedigree of the Sandwith Family of York. Compiled in 1899		1 it.
Smith		
Pedigrees of the Kindred of the Late Henry Smith, Esq., living January, 1898		1
Whittell		
Bennett, John Pedigrees of Members of the Whittell Family from Court Records. Includes the will of William Whittell. (Cheshire Record Office)	1964	1 it.
Woodhull		
Woodhull Family Chart from the College of Arms		1 it.
Wynne		
See Godolphin		

PERSONAL RECORDS: Histories

	Dates Covered	No. of Rolls

FAMILY HISTORIES

Aldis

    Marriage of Daniel Aldis and Mary Dix with Birth
       and Burial Notes of the Aldis Family of
       Tivetshall and Moulton   1761-1838   1 it.

Allport

    Fletcher, W. G. D.
        Abstracts of Deeds and Wills relating to the
        Families of Fletcher and Allport   1 it.

Baildon

    Genealogical Material relating to the Families of
        Baildon, Tinker   1

Bailey

    Mount, Ira William
        Genealogical Research on Ward, Witham, Bailey,
        Tooke, Wright Families   1

Baldwin

    Abstracts of Early English Wills and Administra-
       tions of the Baldwin Family. Copied for
       Evelyn Baldwin, 1 vol. manuscript.
       (Genealogical Society of Utah)   1550-1670

Bemond

    Hardwick, William
        Paternal Remains of the Family of Bemond and
        of the Powells. (Genealogical Society of
        Utah)   1840   1 it.

Benest

    Bernau, Charles Allan
        A Short Account of the Descendants of
        Abraham Benest of Jersey, 1 vol. manuscript

Bennett

    Bennett, John
        Collections on the Bennett Family   3

	Dates Covered	No. of Rolls

Benson

Clay, John William
    Collection of Notes and Abstracts relating
    to the Benson Family   1

Bernard

Paternal Remains of the Family of Bernard and
    of the Powells. (Genealogical Society of
    Utah)   1840   1 it.

Booty

Booty, Harold
    The Booty Family of Norfolk, Australia, and
    the U.S.A. Compiled from the work of
    Charles A. Bernau and the notes and research
    of Harold Booty. Indexed. Later revised
    and published, 1976. (Genealogical Society
    of Utah)   1

Boyd

Boyd, Sir Percival
    Ancestry of Percival Boyd. 1955, 1 vol. manuscript.

Bulkley

Jones, David Cyril
    The Bulkleys of Baron Hill, Anglesey, and
    Cheshire. M.A. Thesis, University College
    of Wales. (National Library of Wales)   1 it.

Charlton

History of Genealogical Records of the Charlton
    Family   1177-1813   1 it.

Clayton

Porter, Sarah Jane Clayton
    Genealogy of the Edward Clayton Family.
    Additional notes in pencil by Melvin
    Clayton of Preston, Idaho   1 it.

Conder

See Kirby.

Constable

Accounts of the Various Branches of the Constable
    Family of Yorkshire. (Yorkshire Archaeological
    Society)   1 it.

	Dates Covered	No. of Rolls

I'Anson, Bryan
    Records of the Constable Family of York and
    the North Country, 1 vol. manuscript.
    (Genealogical Society of Utah)		

Conwayt		

Genealogical Notes with Extracts from Wills and
    Draft Pedigrees of the Conwayt Families of
    Wales, Ireland, and England
		1 it.

Cook		
See Hartle		
Dale		

Dale, Alan
    Local Records of the Dale Family of Cheshire.
    Includes wills, will abstracts, deeds, family
    Bible entries, pedigrees, tax and tithe
    assessments, and parish account books of
    John Norbury. Arranged alphabetically.
    (Worcester Record Office)
		5

Dalton		
Leaming, F. E. The Dalton Book. (British Museum)		1
Dickinson		

Dickinson, Wharton
    Manuscript Records of the Dickinson Family
    of England and Croisadone. (Genealogical
    Society of Pennsylvania)
	1243-1900	1

Ellis		

Ellis Family Notes with letters and pedigrees
    including a History of the Family in
    Jamaica
	1655-1790	2 it.

Eyton		
Genealogical and Historical Records of the Eyton Family		1 it.
Fawcett		

Kendall, H. P.
    Genealogical and Historical Material of the
    Fawcett Family of Yorkshire, Manuscript 649.
    (Yorkshire Archaeological Society)
		1 it.

	Dates Covered	No. of Rolls

Gifford

    Gifford, Walter LeGrande
        The Known History of Stephen and Ann Gifford
        of South Petherton, Somersetshire, England.
        (Genealogical Society of Pennsylvania)   1 it.

Gurney

    Bernau, Charles Allan
        The Gurney Family. 1918, 1 vol. manuscript.
        (Genealogical Society of Utah)

Hartle

    Hartle, Frank
        Original Research for Hartle and Cook Families
        with Branch Lines. Includes 50 years
        research. 1968. (Genealogical Society of Utah)   3 it.

Huish

    Haymore, Emma H.
        An Index of Christian Names of the Surname
        of Huish, 1 vol. manuscript. (Genealogical
        Society of Utah)

Ison

    Ison, Louie S.
        Ison Genealogy of Virginia, Kentucky, and
        England. (Genealogical Society of Utah)   3

Jermyn

    Hunter, Joseph (fl. 1850)
        An Account of the Rishbrooke and Jermyn
        Families and Allied Families of Yorkshire.
        (Yorkshire Archaeological Society)   1 it.

King

    King, Alfred B.
        Genealogy of the Descendants of Robert King
        of Burroughby, Yorkshire. (Genealogical
        Society of Utah)   1630-1950   1 it.

Kirby

    Hunter, Joseph (fl. 1850)
        A Sketch of the Life of the Rev. Joshua Kirby,
        an Ejected Minister . . . and Others relating
        to Wadsworth, Conder and Other Families   1 it.

	Dates Covered	No. of Rolls

Lant

Haymore, F. Lant
    The Family of Lant. Includes copies of birth,
    marriage and death certificates. Indexed.
    (Genealogical Society of Utah)   1837-1961   3

Lippincott

Kendall, H. P.
    Genealogical and Historical Material of the
    Lippincott Family of England and America   1 it.

Marley

Evidences of the Marley Family   1 it.

Minns

Minns, George
    History of the Minns Family, 2 vols.
    manuscript

Norman

Norman, Bertram William Tuff
    Research Papers for a History of the
    Ancestry of Bertram William Tuff Norman,
    1 vol. manuscript

Nuttalls

Hayhurst, T. H.
    The Romance of the Nuttalls, 1 vol. manuscript

Parry

Parry-Perry Family Notes   1910   1 it.

Pearce

Woods, Albert William
    Genealogy of the Family of William Pearce of
    the County of Brecon and the County of
    Gloucestershire. Compiled from records
    at the College of Arms. (National Library
    of Wales)   1

Phillimore

Phillimore, W. P. W.
    The Family of Phillimore, 1 vol. manuscript.
    (Genealogical Society of Utah)   1903

	Dates Covered	No. of Rolls

Phillipps

    Phillipps, Sir Thomas
        Notes and Descendants of Sir Thomas Phillipps of Newton, Limavady. Phillipps Manuscript T377. (Belfast Public Record Office) — 1

Plantagenet

    Moriarty, George Andrews
        Plantagenet Ancestry of Edward III and Queen Philippa. (Historical Society of Pennsylvania) — 1

Powell

    See Bemond

    See Bernard

Pusey

    Miscellaneous Genealogical Notes on Pusey Seymore and other Families from Various English Counties — 1 it.

Rishbrooke

    See Jermyn

Scarborough

    Collections for a History of the Scarborough Family[5]. (Leeds Central Library) — 1693-1713 — 1

Seymore

    See Pusey

Sherwood

    Sherwood, George
        Collections relating to the Surname of Sherwood. (Genealogical Society of Utah) — 7

Skelton

    Hayhurst, T. H.
        Notes on the Skelton Family, 1 vol. manuscript

---

[5]Cataloged under Yorkshire, Leeds, Templenewsam Collection.

	Dates Covered	No. of Rolls

Summerhays

    Minns, George
        Genealogical Records of the Joseph W.
        Summerhays Family of Devonshire.
        (Genealogical Society of Utah)   1

Talbot

    Abstracts of Births, Marriages, and Deaths,   16th-
        with Wills for the Talbot Family. Alphabetical   20th C.   3

    The Coronation Claims of the Earls of Shrewsbury,
        their Origin, Vicissitudes and Present
        Condition.   1 it.

Terrick

    Genealogical Information relating to the Terrick
        and Other Families from England   1 it.

Tooke

    See Bailey

Wadsworth

    See Kirby

Ward

    See Bailey

Weatherhead

    Weatherhead, Edith
        Notes on the Weatherhead Family of Pateley
        Bridge, Yorkshire. Manuscript 676[6].
        (Yorkshire Archaeological Society)   1 it.

Willis

    Willis, H. J.
        Genealogical Collections of the Willis Family.
        (Genealogical Society of Utah)   10

Witham

    See Bailey

Wright

    See Bailey

	Dates Covered	No. of Rolls
LOCAL HISTORIES		
Cookson, Edward Yorkshire Chronicles	1066-1766	1
Fillmore, Gwen The Shire of Durham. Includes maps. 1964, 24 leaves.		
Froucester, Walter Abbot History of St. Peter's Abbey, Gloucester, with a Glossary of Plants, Drugs and Medical Recipes. 1538.		1 it.
Hall, W. T. The Rectors of Desford and Other Village Notes. Indexed.	1209-1897	1 it.
Henderson, Charles G. History of the Hundreds of Kerrier and Powder.		2
A History of the Diocese of Exeter, 1887.		1 it.
History of Welsh Calvinistic Methodists in Birkenhead.		1
Jones, J. Ernest A History of the Calvinistic Methodist Church, Wolverhampton, Staffordshire. With accompanying letters in Welsh. 1913.		1 it.
Kendall, J. G. The Town of Hamilton in Leicestershire and its Ancient Lords.		1 it.
Willis, Naomi The Shire of Essex. 1964.		1 it.
Photos of the Clergy of Hereford with Church Notes.	1832-1879	2 it.

PERSONAL RECORDS: Monumental Inscriptions

	Dates Covered	No. of Rolls

British Mission, L.D.S. Church
  Monumental Inscriptions of England.
    (Genealogical Society of Utah)
		7

Kendall, H. P. Index of Epitaphs in Halifax Parish Churchyard.		1 it.

Longmate
  A Collection of Monumental Inscriptions Selected
  from Monuments and Coffin Plates. Several
  counties. Phillipps Manuscript 11201. (Society
  of Antiquaries)
		1

A List of Monumental Inscriptions in Bedfordshire.		1

Merrill, Max J.
  Index by County of the First 10 Volumes of a
  Supplement to Monumental Inscriptions of the
  British Isles, 1 vol. manuscript, 1966.		

Monumental Inscriptions . . . English-speaking People in Switzerland. (National Library of Wales)	19th & 20th C.	1 it.

Obituary Record Society
  Monumental Inscriptions of England, Ireland,
  Scotland, Wales, and Canada. Compiled under
  the direction of the Genealogical Board of
  the British Mission, L.D.S. Church.
  (Genealogical Society of Utah)
		18

Richardson, W. H.
  Monumental Effigies in England and Wales.
    (Burlington House, Picadilly)
		2

Sherwood, George F. T.
  Monumental Inscriptions of Englishmen Buried
  Abroad: Bellagio, Italy
            Capri
            Florence
            Milan
            Naples
            Berne, Switzerland
            Geneva
            Ouchy
            Mt. Zion, Jerusalem
            Malaya, Spain
            Gibraltar
            Kingston, Jamaica
            Homburg vorder Hohe, Germany
		13 it.

VI RESEARCH AIDS

Throughout this Inventory, where a record had been indexed at the time it was created or transcribed, the notation "indexed" appears in the regular entry (usually under "Papers"). Where an independent calendar or list or index is itself considered an original record, it appears in the various sections as "Indexes."

The section on Research Aids covers those instances where works have been composed at a later date, drawing upon one or more series of documents and/or having in any way rearranged the order or information of such documents. Also included are transcripts, extracts, and abstracts of documents. Most of these were compiled by genealogists and local historians in the process of expediting their own research.

The material covered has been divided into two categories: aids which have been created elsewhere and made part of the collection, and those aids which were created by the Genealogical Society as auxiliaries to the collection. In the first category (Research Aids – General), material is subdivided according to coverage (national, county, local, and other). The second category (Research Aids – Genealogical Society of Utah Guides), which contains some published material, is arranged along the lines of the general classification of the Inventory. The Society's aids include: 1) guides for genealogical research; 2) abstracts and indexes prepared by volunteers under the supervision of the Society's research department; and 3) registers of contents and call numbers for those document series with multiple rolls of film. The registers describe the collection briefly, the years covered, suggestions on how to use the records, and give the roll numbers for each part of the series. Sometimes the records listed in these registers are also cataloged individually under appropriate locality and subject headings. The majority of them are listed only in these registers.

These research aids are available on microfilm and in typewritten form for use in the library.

RESEARCH AIDS: General

	Dates Covered	No. of Rolls
GOVERNMENT RECORDS: National		
Chancery		
Abstracts of Chancery Proceedings, with surname index. Compiled by Charles Allan Bernau	1714-1758	617
How to Use Bernau's Abstracts of Chancery Proceedings. Includes library call numbers, 1 vol.	1714-1758	
Extracts of Pipe Rolls, Fine Rolls, and Patent Rolls chiefly relating to Cornwall and Devon, Henry I to Henry VII, Indexed		1
Guide to Grantees enrolled in records of Court of Chancery	1461-1848	48
Index to Close Rolls relating to several counties of England and Wales	1743-1758	2
Exchequer		
Extracts of Knights' Fees, Cornwall, Indexed	c.1500-1700	1
Registrar-General		
List of Non-Parochial Registers and Records in the Custody of the Registrar-General. Lists and Index Society, vol. 42, interleaved with microfilm call numbers, 1 vol.		
War Office		
Full and Half-pay Officers' Children. WO 25/750-59. Compiled by Charles Allan Bernau, 15 vols. manuscripts	1828	
Soldiers Who Died in the Great War. Compiled from official casualty lists	1914-1919	80
Register of Call Numbers to Soldiers Who Died in the Great War, 3 vols.		
GOVERNMENT RECORDS: Local		
Parochial Vital Records		
Collection of Parish Register and Bishops' Transcripts Extracts. Compiled by William Harold Challen		49

	Dates Covered	No. of Rolls
Register of Call Numbers to the Challen Collection, 1 vol.		
Transcripts of Parish Registers and Monumental Inscriptions. Compiled by George Edward Cokayne	c.1500-1887	11
Phillimore's Parish Register Series of Marriages and Banns		unknown
Register of Contents and Call Numbers to Phillimore's Marriages and Banns, 1 vol.		

Buckinghamshire

	Dates Covered	No. of Rolls
Great Marlow Index to Parish Registers		1

Cambridgeshire

	Dates Covered	No. of Rolls
Baptisms, Marriages, Banns, Burials of the Parishes of Cambridgeshire. Index compiled by T.P.R. Layng. Cataloged individually by parish, 10 vols.		

Cheshire

	Dates Covered	No. of Rolls
Card Index to Bishops' Transcripts	1873-1893	1
Inventory of Transcripts of Lancashire Parish Registers at the Chester Diocesan Registry		1

Devon

	Dates Covered	No. of Rolls
Bishops' Transcripts. Compiled by O.M. Mayer	1507-1800	1 it.

Durham

	Dates Covered	No. of Rolls
Registers of Births, Baptisms, Banns, Marriages, and Burials in Durham County Record Office, May	1968	1 it.
Vital Records of Durham and Northumberland. Compiled by B.W.T. Norman, 27 vols.	1653-1812	

Hampshire

	Dates Covered	No. of Rolls
Registers Deposited at the Portsmouth City Record Office		1 it.

Lancashire

	Dates Covered	No. of Rolls
Index to Giles Shaw's 1889 Printed Register of Oldham Parish and St. Mary's Oldham, 3 vols.	1796-1817	1 it.

	Dates Covered	No. of Rolls
Lincolnshire		
Transcripts of Parish Registers, Collated with Bishops' Transcripts and Quaker Wills. Various years. Compiled by Harold Witty Brace		1 it.
Transcripts of Parish Registers for more than 91 parishes. Compiled by Charles Wilmer Foster. Individually cataloged		91 it.
Oxfordshire		
Index to Oxfordshire Parish Registers. Compiled by Frederick Simon Snell		1
List of Oxfordshire Parish Registers. A Return to the Diocesan Registrar	1813	1 it.
Reports on the Contents of Oxfordshire Parish Chests in the Bodleian Library. Made for the National Register of Archives		1
Northumberland		
A List of Transcripts of Parish Registers of Northumberland and Durham in the Newcastle Public Library		1 it.
Nottinghamshire		
Calendar of Transcripts of Parish Registers of Archdeaconry of Nottingham. Compiled by W.A. James	1598-1871	1
Staffordshire		
Transcripts of Parish Registers and Bishops' Transcripts for Chebsey, Staffs. Compiled by Norman W. Tildesley, 1 vol.	1660-1714	
Suffolk		
An Index to the Parish Registers for 147 Suffolk Parishes. Compiled by R.F. Bullen	1630	1 it.
Sussex		
Parish Registers and Monumental Inscriptions of Sussex. Compiled by George Edward Cokayne		1
Yorkshire		
East Riding Parish Registers in the East Riding County Record Office		1 it.

	Dates Covered	No. of Rolls

North Riding
     List of Parishes for Which Records Have
     Been Deposited in the North Riding
     Record Office, 1972 — 1 it.

West and North Ridings
     Bishops' Transcripts of Parish Registers in
     the Archives Department, Leeds City
     Libraries — 1 it.

Non-parochial Vital Records

Society of Friends

     Collection of Society of Friends Records. Includes
     Births, Marriages, Burials, Monthly and Quarterly
     Meetings, Certificates of Removal. Compiled by
     Gilbert Cope. Individually cataloged — c.1650–1789 — 6

     Lincolnshire

          Index to Quaker Births, Marriages and Deaths,
          and Monthly Meetings in Gainsborough. Compiled
          by Harold Witty Brace — 1654–1837 — 4

          Indexes to Quaker Monthly and Quarterly Meet-
          ings. Compiled by Harold Witty Brace.
          Individually cataloged — 1654–1837 — 10

Other Local Records

Kent

     Folkestone
          Extracts from Town Records. Indexed — 1687–1800 — 1

Norfolk

     Norwich
          Index to Personal Names in the Norwich
          Subscription Books — 1637–1800 — 1 it.

     Yarmouth, Great
          St. Nicholas
               Assembly Book Extracts — 1566–1707 — 1 it.

Shropshire

     Transcript of Domesday Book, County of Salop
     and Marches of Wales. Made by Joseph Morris,
     1 vol. manuscript

	Dates Covered	No. of Rolls
LEGAL RECORDS: Local		
Miscellaneous Forfeitures relating to English and Welsh Popish Recusants. Indexed	1680-1683	1 it.
Cheshire		
Abstracts of Deeds, Lancashire and Cheshire	1500-1800	1
Devon		
Calendar of Deeds in County Devon. Indexed. Compiled by John C. Tingey	1536-1763	2
Essex		
Calendar of Deeds in the County Record Office	1100-1850	9
Lancashire		
Index of Lancashire and Cheshire Depositions. Compiled by James R. M. Glencross, et al	1700-1760	1 it.
Calendar of Lancashire and Cheshire Deeds and Wills in the County Record Office	c.1500-1800	1
Manuscript Inventory of Conveyances and Property Documents Deposited in the County Record Office by Solicitors and Private Families [1]		5
Lincolnshire		

Fleet
   St. Mary Magdalen
      Deed Transcripts
	1621-1783	1 it.

Nottinghamshire		
Executions. Compiled by H. N. Peyton	1750-1850	1
Oxfordshire		
Goring Manor Court Rolls. Transcribed by E. E. Cope, 1 vol. manuscript	1519	
Somersetshire		
Taunton Deane Abstracts from Court Books. Compiled by H. H. Phipps	1636-1720	1 it.

---

[1] Cataloged as "Index of Families" in the Lancashire General File.

	Dates Covered	No. of Rolls

Sussex

Bedam
     Notes from Manor Court Rolls   1 it.

CHURCH RECORDS: Church of England

Marriage Records

Boyd's Marriage Index of England, 1st, 2nd and
3rd Series. Indexed. Compiled by Sir
Percival Boyd   1500–1837   174

Register to Boyd's Marriage Index, 1 vol.

Phillimore's Marriages and Banns of England.
A Supplement to Sir Percival Boyd's Index.
Compiled by W. P. W. Phillimore   unknown

Marriages Extra to the Phillimore Collection.
Compiled by Colliard, Clench, and Mount   1 it.

Chester

Index to Cheshire Marriages. Compiled by
Bertram Merrill   1580–1836   1 it.

Durham

Marriage Bonds. Pt. Indexed. Compiled by
Edwin Dodds   1590–1815   6

Exeter

Crediton
     Marriage Indexes. Compiled by M. A. Furston   1538–1837   2

Gloucester

Index to Marriages of 200 Parishes. Index to
printed parish register volumes compiled by
Eric Arthur Roe   1538–1837   14

Lincoln

Hertfordshire Marriage Index. Compiled by Thomas
F. Allen. "The closest to a complete name index."
Individually cataloged   1538–1838   26

Hertfordshire Marriages. Indexed. Compiled from
parish registers, bishops' transcripts and
marriage licenses   1538–1838   5

	Dates Covered	No. of Rolls
Litchfield and Coventry		
Staffordshire		
Marriage Bonds. Compiled by Norman W. Tildesley, 1 vol. manuscript	1615-1846	
Norwich		
Index to Marriages of Norfolk County. Compiled by Sir Percival Boyd	1500-1837	6
Consistory Court		
Index to Marriage Licenses. Compiled by Walter Rye	1563-1588.	1 it.
Oxford		
Berkshire		
Abstracts of Marriage Bonds;	1616-1846	
Berkshire Peculiars, Great Farrington;	1664-1740	
and Langford	1676-1814	1
Index to Marriages of 139 Parishes in Oxford. Compiled by Jeremy S. W. Gibson [2]	1538-1840	18
Yorkshire		
Paver's Marriage Licenses. Indexes [3]	1567-1777	3
Paver's Marriage Licenses. Brides only, A-Z	c.1590-1599	1 it.
Probate Records		
Canterbury Province		
Abstracts of Wills of Dorset Folk from the Principal Prerogative Court, Canterbury, #1-292. Compiled by George Samuel Fry		4
Index to Stray Wills of the Prerogative Court. Compiled by J. H. Bloom		4
Chichester		
Index of Sussex Wills. From the Drew Collection	1406-1730	1
Durham		
Card Index to Wills in the Newcastle City Archives	16th-19th C.	1

---

[2] Original paper slips and typewritten copy.

[3] A consolidated index for 1567-1630 was printed in the Yorkshire Archaeological Society Journal, Extra Series, II (1912).

	Dates Covered	No. of Rolls
Index or Extracts of Act Books, Wills and Administrations, Consistory Court, Durham and Northumberland. Compiled by John J. Howe	1576–1735	1
Extracts of Durham Wills from the Originals and Early Volumes of Enrollments. Compiled by George Neesham [4]	1540–1725	2

Ely

Calendar of Administrations and Sequestrations from Gibbon's Ely Episcopal Records (Manuscript G.2.IV, Diocesan Registry). Compiled by S. Allyn Peck		1

Exeter

Abstracts of Wills from the Barnstaple Consistory Court, the Prerogative Court of Canterbury and the County of Devon. Compiled by Oswyn Murray	c.1600–1800	20
Index of Testamentary Material in Records of the Principle Registry of the Bishop of Exeter		1 it.

Lichfield and Coventry

Genealogical Abstracts of Wills in the Peculiar Court of Dale Abbey. Indexed. Compiled by Erma Troop	1753–1856	1 it.
List of Wills Proved and Letters of Administration, Manor Court of Court of Sedgley, Staffordshire. Compiled by Norman W. Tildesley, 1 vol. manuscript		

Norwich

Abstracts of Noted Wills and Administrations of the Archdiaconal Court of Sudbury. Indexed. Compiled by T. K. Crossfield	1565–1838	1
Queries on Wills and Administrations at Bury St. Edmonds Commissary Court. Compiled by T. K. Crossfield. These appear to be Crossfield's working notes	1354–1858	1

Salisbury

Extracts of PCC Wills and PCC Admons, from Berkshire. Compiled by Frederick Simon Snell, 1 vol.	1391–1737 1559–1711	5

---

[4] Preface pages state Neesham was more careful in his extracts than "the celebrated historian, Raine."

	Dates Covered	No. of Rolls

Winchester

Extracts of Surrey Wills. Add Manuscript 29609B — 17th–19th C. — 1

York

Yorkshire Will Abstracts. Compiled by Richard Holworthy — — 1 it.

Index to Raine's Transcripts of York Wills. Compiled by James Raine — 1593–1801 — 1

Abstracts of Wills and Administrations of the Peculiar Court of Southwell, Nottinghamshire. Indexed, 1695–1857. Compiled by Erma Troop, 33 vols. — 1567–1857 — 8

CHURCH RECORDS: Nonconformists

Society of Friends (Quakers)

Alphabetical Digest of the Names of over Seven Thousand Women who Petitioned Against Tithes — 1659 — 1 it.

CORPORATE RECORDS

Hampshire

Guide to the Records of the Corporation of Southampton and Absorbed Authorities in the Civil Record Office. Indexed — 1964 — 1 it.

Lancashire

Directory of Foreign Merchants. Compiled by John Scholes — 1784–1870 — 1 it.

Norfolk

Handlist of the Archives of Great Yarmouth Corporation in the Town Clerk's Department which date before 1835, 1 vol.

Yorkshire

Index to the Burgage Book for Pontefract. Compiled by H. P. Kendall — 1767 — 1 it.

PERSONAL RECORDS

Paget, Gerald

Genealogical and Heraldic Baronage of England. An Account of the Ancient Nobility. Surname Index — 1066–1500 — 5

	Dates Covered	No. of Rolls

Phillipps, Sir Thomas

Index Nominum in Libris Dictis, Cole's Escheats
inter Harleian Manuscripts #410-11 and #756-60
Compiled in 1852, 1 vol. manuscript

Durham

The Coleman Deeds, Durham, and Northumberland,
n.d. Indexed. Compiled by H. R. Leighton   1 it.

Ely, Diocese

Calendar of Individuals in the Diocese of Ely.
Compiled from parish registers, wills and
deeds, apprentice indentures, and removal
certificates by George Minns. Indexed   1577-1896   3

Essex

General Index of Personal Names from 1500.
Card Indexed   from 1500   21

Hampshire

Guide to Printed, Typescript, and Transcript
Copies of Monumental Inscriptions of Hampshire
at the Society of Genealogists, London   1 it.

Herefordshire

Card Index to Genealogies in the Hereford
Public Library   1948   1

Lincolnshire

Research Extracts from Canon Foster's Notebooks,
County of Lincoln. Compiled by Charles Wilmer
Foster   12

Norfolk

Alphabetical List of Thousands of Names, mostly
from Norfolk and Suffolk. Compiled by Herbert
Burrell   1 it.

Index to Personal Names in the Norwich Subscrip-
tion Books   1637-1800   1 it.

Northamptonshire

General Index to Personal Names in the County
Record Office   9

	Dates Covered	No. of Rolls
Shropshire		
Card Index to Manuscript Pedigrees in the Shrewbury Public Library		1
The Sheriffs of Shropshire from Blakeway and other Sources. Compiled by William Phillips. Phillips Manuscript 1890		3
Somerset		
Index to Names of Persons in the Card Index of the Somerset Archaeological Society. Compiled by H. R. Phipps	1937	1 it.
RESEARCH AIDS		
Canterbury, Diocese		
Dean and Chapter of Canterbury Catalog of the Archives of the Dean and Chapter	to 1900	3
Cornwall		
Calendars of Cornish Manuscripts. Indexed. Compiled by Charles G. Henderson		12
Card Index of the Muniment Room Records, Royal Institution of Cornwall	1959	2
Dorset		
Calendar of Documents deposited at the Dorset County Museum by the Society of Genealogists, London. Compiled by G. D. Squibb	1941	1 it.
Herefordshire		
Biographical Index at the Hereford Public Library		4
Inventory of Manuscript Collections in the Hereford Public Library [5]		1
Lancashire		
Inventory of Presbyterian Parish Registers of Lancashire and Cheshire, on Deposit in the National Library of Wales. Includes notes on ministers	1624-1855 1717-1731	1

---

[5]Cataloged as "Index of Pilley Collection." The Pilley Collection is just one of those described in the inventory.

	Dates Covered	No. of Rolls

Leicestershire

Schedule of Records Deposited in the City of
Leicester Archives — 4

Records of the Society of Genealogists, London,
held by the Leicestershire County Council — 1 it.

Lincoln, Diocese

A Handlist of the Records of the Archdeaconry
of Leicester. Compiled by C. E. W. in 1951 — 1517-1919 — 1 it.

Litchfield and Coventry, Diocese

Lichfield Diocese Peculiars. Compiled by
Norman W. Tildesley — 1 it.

Worcestershire

Inventory of Records in the County Record
Office — 1964 — 16

York, Diocese

Deanery Book, Archdeacon of Richmond — 1612-1827 — 10 it.

Miscellaneous Guides

Alphabets, Abbreviations, Signs of various
periods, n.d. Compiled by George Minns — 1 it.

Rough Index of Names and Places in the Cheshire
Sheaf, Volumes 1-2, 1st Series. Compiled by
John Bennett — 1 it.

Index to the Gentleman's Magazine. Compiled
by the College of Arms, London, and typed by
the Genealogical Society of Utah, 75 vols. — 1731-1871 — 24

Inventories and Guides to the Manuscript
Collections of the National Library of Wales — 114

Register of Call Numbers for Inventories and
Guides to the Manuscript Collections of the
National Library of Wales, 1 vol.

Index to Surnames in Lancashire Maps giving
the Parishes for which Registers have been
published . . . to 1944 and the number of
times a surname appears in the parish — to 1944 — 4

Index to Christenings, Marriages, and Burials
in the Parish Magazine of Cheshire and
Lancashire. Compiled by B. W. T. Norman — 1870-1941 — 2 it.

RESEARCH AIDS: GENEALOGICAL SOCIETY OF UTAH GUIDES

	Dates Covered	No. of Rolls
GUIDES FOR GENEALOGICAL RESEARCH		
Government Records		
Population Movements in England. Compiled from population tables from the censuses of Great Britain and Index of Places, 1851 census	1821-1851	1 it.
English Militia Records in the Public Record Office and County Record Offices, 1 vol.	1967	
List of Parish Registers of England and Census Records of the United States in the Genealogical Library, Mesa, Arizona. Compiled by Archibald F. Bennett		1 it.
Catalog of Nonconformist Registers deposited at Somerset House, London. Compiled by Ira W. Mount, 1933, 1 vol.		
List of Nonconformist Chapels in England before 1838 including Those of Which no Register Exists, but excluding Jews and Members of the Society of Friends (Quakers), 1 vol.		
Legal Records		
English Quarter Sessions Records in Local Depositories in England, revised edition, 1967, 1 vol.		
List of Known Manor Court Rolls, 1 vol.	1965-1968	
Church Records		
Probate Records Handlist of Pre-1858 Probate Jurisdictions, 1967-1968, 39 vols.	Pre-1858	
Research Aids		
Canals in the British Isles, 1 vol.		
Controlled Extract Evaluation Forms for the Computer File Index. An analysis of the parish registers of England selected for in-put into the data bank		33

	Dates Covered	No. of Rolls
County Keys: References for Genealogical Research in the Counties of Great Britain,[6] 41 vols.		
English Magazines Bound Together. Compiled by John D. Nixon, 1 vol.	1965	
Genealogical Gleanings from England. Partial Surname Index to the Society of Genealogists, London, Card File, 18 vols.	1928-1943	7
Occupations, Mineral Resources and Industries in England as of 1831, compiled from Lewis' Topographical Dictionary of England and Wales, 1 vol.	1965	

ABSTRACTS AND INDEXES

Government Records

An Index to the Regimental Records of the British Army. Compiled by John S. Farmer, 1 vol.	1975	
Index to Poor Law Records in Nottinghamshire,[7] 2 vols.	1977	

Church Records

A New Set of Diocesan Maps. Compiled by James Thomas Law and William F. Francis, 1974, 1 vol.	1864	
Index of Testamentary Material in the Records of the Principal Registry of the Bishop of Exeter. Compiled by Olive M. Moger, 1 vol.	1963	
Calendar of Nottinghamshire Probate Records from the Nottinghamshire Deaneries Act Books, 1 vol.	1688-1731, 1970	

Corporate Records

List of Printed Registers of Universities, Colleges, and Schools of England	1967	1 it.

Personal Records

Pedigree Index of Research for Patrons, n.d. Compiled by the LDS British Mission		8

---

[6]The Research Department is currently revising and expanding these guides.

[7]An index for the City of Nottingham is under preparation.

	Dates Covered	No. of Rolls

A Supplement to Monumental Inscriptions of the
British Isles: An Index by County. Compiled
by Max J. Morrell, 1 vol.   1966

REGISTERS OF CONTENTS AND
CALL NUMBERS

Government Records: National

Board of Trade

Register to Agreements and Crew Lists of
British Merchant Vessels, 1 vol. (1748 rolls)   1857–1860

List of English Apprentice and Freemen
Records, 1 vol.

Registrar General

Register to the Index of Civil Registration
of Births, Marriages, and Deaths for England
and Wales from 1 July, 1837, 2 vols.(1077 rolls)   1837

Register of the Grants of Probate and Letters
of Administration, Principal Probate
Registry, 1 vol. (542 rolls)   1858–1957

War Office

Army Records, 1 vol. (1937 rolls)

Government Records: Local

Parochial Records

Register of the William Harold Challon
Collection of Parish Registers and Bishops'
Transcripts, 1 vol. (49 rolls)

Register of the Contents of 27 Volumes of
Christenings and Marriages for Durham and
Northumberland, extracted by B. W. T.
Norman. Compiled by Ronald E. Cunningham,
1 vol. (27 rolls)   1653–1812

Register of Contents to Phillimore's Parish
Register Series of Marriages and Banns.
Compiled by Ronald E. Cunningham, 1 vol.

Register of Staffordshire Parish Records
and Directories in the Genealogical Society
of Utah   1 it.

Register of Bishops' Transcripts for the
Diocese of Worcester, 1 vol. (496 rolls)

	Dates Covered	No. of Rolls

Legal Records

Chancery

How to Use Bernau's Abstracts of Chancery
Proceedings, 1 vol.   1714-1758

Quarter Sessions Records Available at the e
Genealogical Society of Utah, 1 vol.

Church Records

Marriage Records

A Key to the Parishes in Boyd's Marriage
Index, 2nd and 3rd Series. Compiled by
Claire T. Wells, 1 vol.

Register to Boyd's Marriage Index, 1st,
2nd and 3rd Series, 1 vol. (174 rolls)

Register to the Records of the Prerogative
Court of Canterbury, all classes.   1 it.

Canterbury Province

Register of Marriage Allegations and Calendars
of Marriage Licenses, Faculty Office of the
Archbishop of Canterbury. Compiled by   1632-1851
Genevieve Hickison, 1 vol. (217 rolls)   1632-1955

Register to the Marriage Allegations, Vicar
General, Archbishop of Canterbury, and   1660-1851
Indexes, 1 vol. (252 rolls)   1660-1921

Lichfield and Coventry

Marriage Licenses, Bonds, and Allegations,
1 vol. (458 rolls)   1636-1880

Worcester

Marriage Bonds and Allegations. Compiled
by Barbara A. Davies, 1 vol. (359 rolls)   1660-1957

Indexes to the Calendar of Marriage Bonds,   1553-1645
and Index Libri Allegationem Matrimonalium.   1666-1671   2

Probate Records

Chester

Register to Wills and Administrations for
Lancashire in the Cheshire Episcopal
Consistory Court, 1 vol. (1204 rolls)   1846-1858

	Dates Covered	No. of Rolls

Worcester

    Register to Calendar of Wills and Administrations from Indexes to the Act Books of the Episcopal Consistory Court of the Bishop of Worcester, 4 vols. (616 rolls)   1661-1858

Corporate Records

    British East Company

    Register to the Collection of Ecclesiastical Returns and Testamentary Records, 1 vol. (1281 rolls)

Research Aids

    National Library of Wales

    Register of Record Inventories to the Manuscript Collections of the National Library of Wales, 1 vol. (114 rolls)

    Soldiers who Died in the Great War. Compiled from official casualty lists, 3 vols. (80 rolls)   1914-1919

VII LONDON

The collection of London records comprises the richest and broadest assortment of records within the English collection. More records of a local nature were generated and preserved within the ancient city of London and its neighboring communities than elsewhere. Microfilm access to these records has been good, although limitations on filming of parochial records have been imposed occasionally.

The cataloging of such a massive body of material has its special difficulties. For example, "London" may be thought of as the old city by itself, as the old city plus the adjoining boroughs, or as the modern, metropolitan area. The last has been taken as the definition of London for the Society's cataloging purposes; hence "London" includes all of Middlesex and portions of Essex, Hertford, Kent, and Surrey. Cards are filed by the political boundaries of 1974, then by record classification, and finally in alphabetical order of present-day civil parishes.[1]

This section applies to the London records the general categories of the six previous sections; and it adds a special chart for local government records, designed to indicate at a glance what classes of material may be found for each parish.

---

[1]For modern political boroughs, see Bartholomew's Reference Atlas of Greater London, 13th ed., 1968, repr., 1972; for current civil parishes, see Parish Registers: A Handlist. London: Guildhall, 1967 (3 vols); for further information on merged or altered jurisdictions, see London Parishes. Salt Lake City: Genealogical Society, 1971.

GOVERNMENT RECORDS: City

	Dates Covered	No. of Rolls
CITY OF LONDON		
Papers		
Common Sargeants Book. In Latin	1586-1741	5
Lists of non-Freemen. n.d.		1 it.
List of the Lord Mayors and a Number of the Sheriffs	1232-1623	1 it.
Taxes Assessed on Births, Marriages and Burials. (The records suggest that the tax was levied independently of vital events as a variant of the poll taxes. Cataloged only under London, Southwark, Holborn, and Camden.)	1695	6
Indexes		
Hustings Rolls, Index of Names, A-Z.		2

GOVERNMENT RECORDS: Local

	Dates Covered	No. of Rolls
VITAL RECORDS		
Papers		
Chelsea Hospital		
Baptisms, Marriages, and Burials	1691-1856	2
London Diocese		
International Registers of Births, Marriages, and Burials of British Subjects	1816-1878	4
Original Certificates of Baptisms and Marriages of British Subjects Abroad	1816-1870	7
Royal Naval Hospital, Greenwich		
Baptisms, Marriages, and Burials	1720-1857	2

Frequency Tables

The Genealogical Society's Parish and Vital Records Listings give a comprehensive and detailed account of which parish registers and bishops' transcripts are in its holdings. The coverage for each London borough is summarized in the following tables. Also included are some unofficial transcripts, since the catalog cards do not always differentiate between original registers and copies made from them. Thus, the first table shows frequency distribution of parish registers and bishops' transcripts for the boroughs of Greater London, as counted under every half century. Items include births, christenings, marriages, deaths, and burials. The second table shows frequency distribution of vital information recorded by Nonconforming churches, alms houses, workhouses, schools, and other institutions.

Parochial Registers and Bishops' Transcripts

BOROUGH	to 1550	1550-1599	1600-1649	1650-1699	1700-1749	1750-1799	1800-1849	1850-1899	1900-
Barking			2						
Barnett		1	5	4	4	7	8	2	
Bexley									
Brent			1						
Bromley	1	1	1	6	1	8	9		
Camden		1	2	4	6	6	9	18	7
Croydon				3	1	5	10	3	
Ealing		1	4	5	2	3	3	3	
Enfield			2				2	3	
Greenwich			1	1	3	3	9	14	2
Hackney	1	3	4	4	3	6	12	11	4
Hammersmith							1	2	1
Haringey			1	1	1	1	2	2	1
Harrow			3	2	2	3	3	1	
Havering		4	5	4	5	4	4		
Hillingdon		2	8	3	3	4	4	3	
Hounslow		6	1	2	4	3	2		
Ilford-Redbridge						1	1	1	
Islington			1		1	3	7	9	
Kensington and Chelsea		1	3	3	3	4	5	9	2
Kingston upon Thames	1	1	1	4	3	3	6	3	
Lambeth				1	1	1	13	12	7
Lewisham		2	2	2	4	3	9	11	5
London City	32	73	112	107	93	97	115	73	33
Merton				2	1	3	9	2	
Newham	1	1	2	1	1	1	1	2	2
Richmond upon Thames			3	3		5	8	2	
Southwark		2	7	6	6	13	45	34	17
Sutton									
Tower Hamlets		4	10	9	13	15	23	37	10
Waltham Forest								1	1
Wandsworth			1	4	2	4	9	7	1
Westminster		3	6	5	7	8	15	20	7

Non-parochial Registers

BOROUGH	to 1550	1550–1599	1600–1649	1650–1699	1700–1749	1750–1799	1800–1849	1850–1899	1900–
Barking				3	3	4	4		
Barnett				1	1		1	4	2
Bexley							1		
Brent									
Bromley				2	3	3	2		
Camden				1	4	9	20	6	5
Croydon				1	1	2	3	1	1
Ealing									
Enfield				1	2	2	9		
Greenwich						5	17	5	1
Hackney					3	8	15	2	1
Hammersmith				1	1	5	6	2	1
Haringey					1	2	4	1	1
Harrow							1		
Havering				1	1		3		
Hillingdon				1	1	3	4	1	
Hounslow						1	2		
Ilford–Redbridge									
Islington			1	1	1	9	28	5	5
Kensington and Chelsea									
Kingston upon Thames			1	2	2	4	4	1	
Lambeth						3	22	4	4
Lewisham						2	8		2
London City	0	5	8	21	22	48	48	16	2
Merton									
Newham						2	3	1	
Richmond upon Thames					1	1	2	1	1
Southwark			1	7	8	15	33	9	2
Sutton									
Tower Hamlets			4	16	17	27	38	8	3
Waltham Forest						2	2	1	1
Wandsworth			1	1	2	3	7	1	1
Westminster				11	20	25	35	5	3

CITY OF LONDON PARISHES

The wealth of local source material for London is summarized on the following charts. They are arranged alphabetically, first by modern borough, then by political or civil parish with ecclesiastical parishes and independent jurisdiction as sublistings. These correspond roughly to the entries in the Society's card catalog. Where the catalog entry follows the exact title of the record it has been noted for access.

The "Poor Law" heading spans the columns: Apprenticeship, Pauper Lists, Rate Books, Settlement Records, Workhouse Records.

PARISHES: CITY OF LONDON	Burials	Census Returns	Churchwardens' Accounts	Day Books	Election Records	Inhabitants' Lists	Marriage Allegations	Monumental Inscriptions	School Registers	Tax Records	Vestry Records	Apprenticeship	Pauper Lists	Rate Books	Settlement Records	Workhouse Records	Miscellaneous	Dates
Within the Walls--																		
St Alban, Woodstreet, with St Olave, Silverstreet	*		*			*					*							1583–1841
Allhallows, Barking																		
Allhallows, Breadstreet with St John Evangelist																		
Allhallows the Great and the Less	*		*								*							1616–1708
Allhallows, Lombardstreet								*			*							1667–1841
Allhallows, Staining	*		*	*							*							1491–1787
Allhallows on the Wall with St Augustine	*					*		*	*									1780–1863
St Alphage	*		*			*	*											1527–1668,1840–
St Andrew Undershaft with St Mary Axe						*		*									*	1744–1950
St Andrew by the Wardrobe with St Anne, Blackfrairs																		
St Anne and St Agnes with St John Zachary	*		*		*	*					*					*		1591–1847
St Antholin with St John the Baptist																		
St Augustine, Watlingstreet with St Faith																		1601–1737
St Bartholonew by Royal Exchange																		
St Bene't Fink						*					*							1787–1808
St Bene't Gracechurch with St Leonard Eastcheap	*		*							*								1492–1883
St Bene't, Paul's Wharf, with St Peter	*		*								*							1605–1656,1798
St Botolph, Billingsgate with St George, Botolphlane																		
Christchurch with St Leonard Foster-Lane														*				1574–1698
St Clement, Eastcheap with St Martin Orgors																		
St Dionis Backchurch						*		*			*							1730–1875
St Dunstan in the East			*								*							1494–1651
St Edmund the King with St Nicholas Acons						*					*							1723–1804
St Ethelburga	*		*															1569–1681,
St Helen, Bishopsgate			*			*					*							1565–1835
St James, Duke's Place							*											1707

PARISHES: CITY OF LONDON (continued)	Burials	Census Returns	Churchwardens' Accounts	Day Books	Election Records	Inhabitants' Lists	Marriage Allegations	Monumental Inscriptions	School Registers	Tax Records	Vestry Records	Poor Law: Apprenticeship	Poor Law: Pauper Lists	Poor Law: Rate Books	Poor Law: Settlement Records	Poor Law: Workhouse Records	Miscellaneous	Dates
St James, Garlickhithe																		
St Katherine Coleman						*												1763–1865
St Katherine Creechurch	*	*																1650–1691
St Lawrence, Jewry with St Mary Magdalene, Milkstreet	*	*	*															1518–1657
St Magnus with St Margaret New Fishstreet	*	*				*												1576–1790
St Margaret, Lothbury with St Christopher le Stocks										*								1798–1800
St Margaret Pattens with St Gabriel Fenchurch			*															1506–1794
St Martin, Ludgate																		
St Martin Outwich																		
St Mary Abchurch with St Laurence Putney	*	*																1530–1681
St Mary, Aldermanbury with St Thomas						*												1758–1882
St Mary Aldermary with St Thomas Apostle and St John Baptist upon Walbrook	*	*			*	*												1578–1851
St Mary le Bow with Allhallows Honeylane and St Pancras Soperlane				*		*				*							*	1766–1881
St Mary at Hill with St Andrew Hubbard				*							*			*				1454–1754
St Mary Magdalene, Old Fishstreet with St Gregory by St Paul		*																1673–1728
St Mary Somerset with St Mary Mounthaw	*	*																1614–1794
St Mary Woolnoth with St Mary Woolchurch Haw					*	*												1692–1842
St Matthew, Fridaystreet with St Peter Westcheap	*	*								*								1453–1601,1678
St Michael Bassieshaw																		1669–1753
St Michael Cornhill						*												1800–1880
St Michael Crookedlane						*												1738–1790
St Micheal Queenhythe with Trinity the Less		*				*												1625–1869
St Michael Paternoster Royal with St Martin Vintry								*										n.d.
St Michael Woodstreet with St Mary Staining																		

PARISHES: CITY OF LONDON (continued)	Burials	Census Returns	Churchwardens' Accounts	Day Books	Election Records	Inhabitants' Lists	Marriage Allegations	Monumental Inscriptions	School Registers	Tax Records	Vestry Records	Poor Law Apprenticeship	Pauper Lists	Rate Books	Settlement Records	Workhouse Records	Miscellaneous	Dates
St Mildred Breadstreet with St Margaret Moses																		
St Mildred Poultry with St Mary Colechurch																		
St Nicholas Cole Abbey with St Nicholas Olave								*										1600-1900
St Olave Hartstreet with St Nicholas in the Shambles							*											1701-1840
St Olave, Old Jewry with St Martin Ironmongerlane																		
St Peter Cornhill						*					*							1570-1885
St Peter le Poor																		
St Stephen, Colemanstreet			*								*						*	1486-1881
St Stephen Wallbrook with St Bene't Sherehog			*	*						*	*							1474-1877
St Swithin, Londonstone with St Mary Bothaw			*								*			*				1602-1899
St Vedast Foster with St Michael le Quern			*								*						*	1717-1873
Without the Walls--																		
St Andrew Holborn	*					*						*						1760-1842
St Peter, Saffron Hill																		
Trinity Chapel, Gray's Inn Road																		
St Bartholonew the Great						*												
St Bartholonew the Less				*														
St Botolph, without Aldersgate			*			*				*	*							1466-1679,1811-1890
St Botolph, Aldgate	*		*		*					*	*						*	1558-1953
St Botolph, with Bishopsgate																		
All Saints Chapel																		
St Bride			*			*						*						
Trinity District Ch.																		1713-1851
St Dunstan in the West	*		*			*						*						1516-1943
St Giles without Cripplegate																		
St Sepulchre					*	*						*	*				*	1685-1865
Trinity in the Minories							*	*										1707,1900

PARISHES: CITY OF LONDON (continued)	Burials	Census Returns	Churchwardens' Accounts	Day Books	Election Records	Inhabitants' Lists	Marriage Allegations	Monumental Inscriptions	School Registers	Tax Records	Vestry Records	Poor Law: Apprenticeship	Poor Law: Pauper Lists	Poor Law: Rate Books	Poor Law: Settlement Records	Poor Law: Workhouse Records	Miscellaneous	Dates
Adjacent to the City--																		
St George the Martyr																		
St George, Bloomsbury																		
Trinity Church, Woburn Sq																		
St Giles in the Fields																		
St Peter ad Vincula, Tower																		
Westminster--																		
St Anne, Soho	*											*	*					1686-1851
St Clement Danes	*											*	*	*				1640-1851
St George Hanover Sq	*												*					
Grosvenor Chapel																		1775-1874
Hanover District Ch.																		
St Marks District Chapel																		
St Peters Pimlico																		
St George, Fulham Road																*		1879-1899
St James Picadilly													*					1830-1851
Archbishop Tennison Ch																		
St Philips Chapel																		
St Margarets Chapel																		
St James Berwickstreet																		
York Street Chapel																		
St James Hampstead Rd																		
St John Millbank								*										
Trinity Ch, Knightsbridge							*											1667-69,1800-
St John Baptist, Savoy																		
St John Evangelist, Drury Ln																		
St John Evangelist, Smith Sq																		
St Luke, Berwick St																		
St Margaret																		1561-1875
Broadway Chapel						*							*	*				
St Martin in the Fields						*			*				*	*	*		*	1664-1852
St Matthew Spring Garden																		
Burleigh Chapel																		
St Mary le Strand												*	*	*				1739-1910
St Marylebone	*	*	*	*			*	*					*			*	*	1707-1864
All Souls, Laugham Road																		1825-1875
St Andrew																		
Holy Trinity																		
St Thomas, Portman Sq																		
Mayfair, Mount St																*		1874-1884

PARISHES: CITY OF LONDON (continued)	Burials	Census Returns	Churchwardens' Accounts	Day Books	Election Records	Inhabitants' Lists	Marriage Allegations	Monumental Inscriptions	School Registers	Tax Records	Vestry Records	Poor Law Apprenticeship	Pauper Lists	Rate Books	Settlement Records	Workhouse Records	Miscellaneous	Dates
Paddington					*					*				*		*	*	1830–1897
Holy Trinity																		
St James																		
St Paul, Covent Garden														*	*			1781–1851
St Peter, Great Windmill St																		
St Thomas, Regent St																		
Westminster								*										1772–1899
Holy Trinity, Brompton																		
Buckingham Palace Road																*		1888–1893
Poland St																*		1869–1908

METROPOLITAN PARISHES

The parishes which are part of Greater London are cataloged under the current political borough in which they are located. Cross-reference cards will alert the researcher. Entries under Essex, Hertford, Kent, and Surrey should also be checked for those parishes which were originally part of these counties. There are no separate entries for Middlesex.

Current political boroughs:

Barking	Hackney	Lambeth
Barnett	Haringey	Lewisham
Bexley	Harrow	Merton
Brent	Havering	Newham
Bromley	Hillingdon	Richmond Upon Thames
Camden	Hounslow	Southwark
Croydon	Ilford-Redbridge	Sutton
Ealing	Islington	Tower Hamlets
Enfield	Kensington and Chelsea	Waltham Forest
Fulham	Kingston Upon Thames	Wandsworth
Greenwich		

Those parishes which fall into two or more modern boroughs are listed under both in the card catalog. For example, St. Leonard's, Streatham, will be found both under Lambeth and under Southwark. On the summary charts, they are listed only once.

METROPOLITAN PARISHES*	Burials	Census Returns	Churchwardens' Accounts	Day Books	Election Records	Inhabitants' Lists	Marriage Allegations	Monumental Inscriptions	School Registers	Tax Records	Vestry Records	Poor Law					Miscellaneous	Dates
												Apprenticeship	Pauper Lists	Rate Books	Settlement Records	Workhouse Records		
Barking																		
Dagenham																		
Barnet																		
Barnet (East)			*											*	*		*	1731–1881
Edgware								*										1700–1900
Finchley								*										1700–1900
Friern Barnet																		
Hadley																		
Hendon														*		*		1886–1900
South Mimms																		
Totteridge																		
Whetstone																		
Bexley																		
Erith																		
Brent																		
Kingsbury																		
Willesden																		
Bromley																		
Anerley																*		1843–1866
Bletchingly																		
Hayes																		
Orpington																		
St Mary Cray with Putney																		
Camden																		
Bloomsbury																*		1883–1898
Camden																	*	
St Andrew																		
Broad Street																		
St Giles with St George																*		1869–1879
St Lukes, City Road																*		1869–1901
St Peter, Regent Sq																		
Cleveland St Sick Asylum	*															*		1875–1901
Hampstead		*						*								*		1671–1904

*Includes infirmaries
hospitals, soldiers' homes

METROPOLITAN PARISHES (continued)	Burials	Census Returns	Churchwardens' Accounts	Day Books	Election Records	Inhabitants' Lists	Marriage Allegations	Monumental Inscriptions	School Registers	Tax Records	Vestry Records	Poor Law					Miscellaneous	Dates
												Apprenticeship	Pauper Lists	Rate Books	Settlement Records	Workhouse Records		
Holborn																		1869–1889
St Andrew																		
Endell St Hospital																*		1749–1914
St Giles in the Field													*				*		1727–1823
St George Martyr																	*		1843–1903
Holy Trinity, Kingsway																		
St Sepulchre																		
Kentish Town																		
Lincoln's Inn																		
St Pancras				*												*	*	*	1778–1881
High Gate																	*		1870
Croydon									*										1700–1900
Coulsdon									*										1700–1950
Farleigh																		
Purley																		
Sanderstead									*										1700–1950
Shoreham																		
Ealing																		
Acton																		
Greenford									*										1700–1900
Hanwell										*					*	*			
Northolt									*										1700–1900
Norwood																		
Perivale									*										1700–1900
Enfield																		
Edmonton																		
St Paul																		
Southgate Iron																		
Weld Chapel																		
Enfield																		
St Andrew											*								1777–1796
Ponders End																		
Southgate																		
Winchmorehill																		
Greenwich																		
Charlton																		
Eltham																		
Holy Trinity																		
St John																		

METROPOLITAN PARISHES (continued)	Burials	Census Returns	Churchwardens' Accounts	Day Books	Election Records	Inhabitants' Lists	Marriage Allegations	Monumental Inscriptions	School Registers	Tax Records	Vestry Records	Poor Law Apprenticeship	Pauper Lists	Rate Books	Settlement Records	Workhouse Records	Miscellaneous	Dates
Greenwich																		
St Alphage																*		1848–1901
Greenwich Hospital	*															*		1705–1869
Royal Naval Asylum	*															*		1807–1824
Woolwich								*								*		1871–1901
Hackney																		
Clapton																		
Hackney																*		1791,1845–1865
Church End													*					1836
Holywell													*					1764–1835
St John														*				1785–1845
Sidney Road																*		1874–1901
Hoxton													*					1835–1851
Shoreditch													*			*	*	1688–1893
St John																		
St Leonard																*		1851–1901
St Marks, Old St																		
St Peter, Hoxton Sq																		
St Thomas Sq																		
Hammersmith																		
Fulham																*		1879–1901
All Saints								*										1750–1910
St Paul								*	*						*	*	*	1810–1837
Haringey																		
Highgate								*								*		1834–1900
Whittington Hospital																*		1870–1888
Hornsey																		
Tottenham																		
Harrow																		
Harrow-on-the-Hill								*										1700–1900
Peckham (East)																		
Pinner								*										
Stanmore								*										1700–1900
Terling																		
Havering																		
Hornchurch																		
Romford																		
Upminster																		
Wennington																		

METROPOLITAN PARISHES (continued)	Burials	Census Returns	Churchwardens' Accounts	Day Books	Election Records	Inhabitants' Lists	Marriage Allegations	Monumental Inscriptions	School Registers	Tax Records	Vestry Records	Poor Law					Miscellaneous	Dates
												Apprenticeship	Pauper Lists	Rate Books	Settlement Records	Workhouse Records		
Hillingdon								*										1700–1900
Cowley								*										1700–1900
Drayton (West)													*					1819–1870
Harefield								*										1700–1900
Harlingdon								*										1700–1900
Harmondsworth																		
Hayes								*										1700–1900
Ickenham								*										1700–1900
Northwood								*										n.d.
Ruislip								*									*	1595
Uxbridge																		
Hounslow																		
Brentford																		
Chiswick								*										1700–1900
Cranford								*										n.d.
Feltham																		
Hanworth																		
Heston								*										1700–1900
Isleworth*																		
Islington																		
Clerkenwell								*										n.d.
Finsbury					*													1820–1875
St Luke, Old St	*							*				*	*					1733–1875
St Mary Charterhouse																		
St Paul																		
St Thomas Charterhouse																		
Highbury																		
Holloway																		
Islington	*																*	1713–1900
St Barnabas																	*	1897–1899
Highgate Hill																	*	1867–1901
St Mary																	*	1886–1872
Shadwell Road																		
Kingsland																		
Pentonville																		

*Records partially destroyed by fire.

METROPOLITAN PARISHES (continued)	Burials	Census Returns	Churchwardens' Accounts	Day Books	Election Records	Inhabitants' Lists	Marriage Allegations	Monumental Inscriptions	School Registers	Tax Records	Vestry Records	Poor Law						Dates
												Apprenticeship	Pauper Lists	Rate Books	Settlement Records	Workhouse Records	Miscellaneous	
Kensington–Chelsea																		
Chelsea												*	*		*	*	*	1891–1898
St John Baptist																		
St Luke													*	*	*			1733–1837
Kensington																		
St Anne																		
St Mary																		
Soho																		
Notting Hill																		
St John																		
St Mark																		
Kingston upon Thames								*										1700–1900
Chessington																		
Malden																		
Malden (New)																		
Lambeth																		
Brixton																		
Clapham								*										1700–1950
Holy Trinity								*	*									n.d.
Saint John Evangelist								*										n.d.
Kennington																		
St James																		
St Mark																		
Lambeth								*				*						1761–1856
All Saints																		
St Andrew																		
St Anne																		
St Barnabas																		
St John Evangelist																		
St Mary, Renfrew Road								*								*	*	1854–1919
Rinces Road																*		1850–1870
Norwood																		
Southville																		
Stockwell																		
Streatham								*										1700–1950
St Anne																*		1892–1914
St Leonard																		
Tooting Bec																		
Vauxhall																		
West Norwood	*																	1838–1919

METROPOLITAN PARISHES (continued)	Burials	Census Returns	Churchwardens' Accounts	Day Books	Election Records	Inhabitants' Lists	Marriage Allegations	Monumental Inscriptions	School Registers	Tax Records	Vestry Records	Poor Law					Miscellaneous	Dates
												Apprenticeship	Pauper Lists	Rate Books	Settlement Records	Workhouse Records		
Lewisham_m																	*	1894–1900
Deptford_{ddd}			*															1845–1837
All Saints											*							n.d.
St Mark																		
St Nicholas																		
St Paul																		
Lee																		
Lewisham																		
St Mary with All Saints								*										1700–1950
St Mary with Oxted								*										n.d.
St Philip																		
Sydenham																		
All Angels																		
St Bartholonew																		
St Michael																		
Merton																		
Merton								*										1800–1950
St Paul								*	*									1800–1950
St Peter								*	*									1800–1950
Mitcham								*										1700–1950
Morden																		
Wimbledon																		
Newham																		
East Ham																		
Little Ilford																		
West Ham																		
Redbridge–Ilford																		
Ilford																		
Richmond upon Thames																		
Barnes								*										1700–1900
East Malling																		
Hampton Wick																		
Kew																		
Mortlake																		
Petersham																		
Richmond								*										n.d.
Teddington																		
Twickenham																		

METROPOLITAN PARISHES (continued)	Burials	Census Returns	Churchwardens' Accounts	Day Books	Election Records	Inhabitants' Lists	Marriage Allegations	Monumental Inscriptions	School Registers	Tax Records	Vestry Records	Poor Law — Apprenticeship	Poor Law — Pauper Lists	Poor Law — Rate Books	Poor Law — Settlement Records	Poor Law — Workhouse Records	Miscellaneous	Dates
Southwark	*											*				*		1739–1851
Bermondsey																		
St James								*										1700–1900
St John																*		1791–1806
St Mary Magdalene								*								*		1650–1800
St Olave															*	*		1767–1890
Tanner St																		
Camberwell																		
Dulwich College																		
St George																		
St Giles			*												*		*	1671–1839
Gordon Road																*		1879–1901
Havil St																*		1837–1895
St Philip Apostle																		
Dulwich																		
Fleet Prison																*		1667–1754
Herne Hill																		
Horsleydown												*						1824–1870
Newington									*							*	*	1875–1896
All Saints																		
St Andrew																		
Holy Trinity																		
St Mary																*		1836–1906
St Matthew																		
Nunhead	*																	1840–1871
Peckham											*						*	1866–1939
Rotherhithe																		
All Saints																		
Christ Church																		
Holy Trinity																		
St Mary															*			1789–1790,1812
St Saviour							*									*		1760–1887
Southwark							*											1700–1900
Christ Church	*	*					*	*								*		1821–1945
Emmanuel																		
St George																*		1870–1901
St George Martyr				*														1760–1772
Mint Street																*		1892–1900
St Olaves							*											n.d.
St Paul																		
St Thomas							*											n.d.

METROPOLITAN PARISHES (continued)	Burials	Census Returns	Churchwardens' Accounts	Day Books	Election Records	Inhabitants' Lists	Marriage Allegations	Monumental Inscriptions	School Registers	Tax Records	Vestry Records	Poor Law					Miscellaneous	Dates
												Apprenticeship	Pauper Lists	Rate Books	Settlement Records	Workhouse Records		
Walworth																	*	1910–1924
St John																		
St Peter																		
St Stephen																		
Sutton*																		
Beddington																		
Carshalton								*										n.d.
Effingham																		
Tower Hamlets																		
Bethnal-Green								*	*			*						1729–1878
St Andrew																		
St Matthew								*						*				1818–1833
Waterloo Road																*		1869–1907
Well St																*		1891–1900
Blackwell													*					
Bow		*							*					*		*		1773–1860
St Marylebow														*				1866–1869
Stratford le bow																		
Bromley									*							*		1630,1744–1907
Limehouse												*				*		1838–1863
St George in the East	*								*								*	1729–1875
Norton Folgate																		
Old Ford																		
Poplar		*		*				*	*			*				*		1705–1899
St Mathias																		
Shadwell	*			*										*		*		1663–1837
Spitalfields														*			*	1700
Stepney			*			*	*									*		1703–1719
All Saints																		
Bancroft Road																*		1847–1901
Charles St																*		1864–1892
St Dunstan							*											1707
St George			*													*		1789–1891
St John Evang																		
St Mary																		
Mile End, Old Town																		
St Peter																		
St Philip																		
Ratcliff																		
Southgrove																		
St Thomas								*										1900

METROPOLITAN PARISHES (continued)	Burials	Census Returns	Churchwardens' Accounts	Day Books	Election Records	Inhabitants' Lists	Marriage Allegations	Monumental Inscriptions	School Registers	Tax Records	Vestry Records	Poor Law					Miscellaneous	Dates
												Apprenticeship	Pauper Lists	Rate Books	Settlement Records	Workhouse Records		
Wappingg																		
St John																	*	1848–1851
Raine St																	*	1891–1899
Whitechapel																	*	1877–1901
St Jude																		
St Mary										*								1805–1806
St Mary Matfellow																		
Old Artillery Ground										*						*	*	1771–1865
Waltham Forest																	*	1869–1901
Leytonstone																	*	1879–1904
Walthamstow																		
Wandsworth																		
Battersea								*									*	1854–1890
Putney							*											1700–1900
Summerstone																		
Tooting Graveney																		
Wandsworth							*											1700–1900
All Saints																		
Castle St																	*	1772–1837
St John's Hill																	*	1866–1886
Swaffield Road																	*	1884–1900
Windlesham																		

	Dates Covered	No. of Rolls
BURIAL GROUNDS		
Papers		
Islington		
Bunhill Fields Cemetery, City Road[2]		
Burial Registers	1713-1854	13
Register of Tombstones	1841-1854	1 it.
City of London		
City of London Cemetery, Little Ilford		
Register of Monuments, n.d.		2
Inscriptions of Monuments of those Interred from the Parishes of St. Peter le Poor and St. Benet Fink, n.d.		1 it.
Register of Burials	1856-1915	58
Lambeth		
South Metropolitan Cemetery		
Burials	1838-1919	15
Southwark		
Nunhead Cemetery		
Burials	1840-1871	4
Union Street, Deadman's Place Cemetery		
Burials	1739-1837	2 it.
Tower Hamlets		
Burial Dues	1841	1
Indexes		
Islington		
Bunhill Fields Cemetery		
Books of Interment	1823-1854	2 it.

OTHER JURISDICTIONS

The records for Liberties, Poor Law Unions and Wards are summarized on the charts which follow.

---

[2]Records for the Quaker Burial Ground, Royal Alexandra and Albert School, Dissenters Burial Ground and London Ministers are also in the Collection. They are individually cataloged by title or denomination.

LIBERTIES	Burials	Census Returns	Churchwardens' Accounts	Day Books	Election Records	Inhabitants' Lists	Marriage Allegations	Monumental Inscriptions	School Registers	Tax Records	Vestry Records	Poor Law — Apprenticeship	Poor Law — Pauper Lists	Poor Law — Rate Books	Poor Law — Settlement Records	Poor Law — Workhouse Records	Miscellaneous	Dates
Without the Walls—																		
Barnard's Inn																		
Bridewell Hospital																		
Bridewell Precinct	*																	1681
Clifford's Inn																		
Furnival's Inn																		
Gray's Inn																		
Inner Temple																		
Lincoln's Inn																		
Middle Temple																		
Serjeant's Inn, Chy Lane																		
Staple Inn																		
White Friar's Precinct						*												1810
Adjacent to London—																		
St Catherine by the Tower Precinct																		
Charter-House																		
East Smithfield																		
Ely-Place																		
Ely-Rents																		
Hatton Gardens																		
Norton-Falgate																		
Old Artillery Ground																		
Old Tower Without																		
Saffron Hill																		
Westminster—																		
Close of the Collegiate Church of St Peter																		
Duchy of Lancaster																		
Liberty of the Rolls*													*	*				1762-1851
Precinct of the Savoy														*				1850-1851
Privy Gardens																		
The Verge of St James and Whitehall																		
Wellington Barracks, Royal Chapel																	*	1882
Whitehall																		

*Cataloged under Westminster

POOR LAW UNIONS	School Records				Poor Law Records					Workhouse Records[1]						Dates
	Apprenticeship	Creed Registers	Death Registers	School Registers	Apprenticeship	Bastardy	Pauper Lists	Rate Books	Settlement Records	Admissions	Apprenticeship	Creed Registers	Discharges	Residents	Vital Statistics	
Bethnal-Green											*				*	1876–1900
Bermondsey															*	1836–1870
Camberwell																
Chelsea aaa		*								*			*	*		1851–1901
Edmonton																
Greenwich	*	*	*	*						*	*				*	1845–1902
Hackney		*	*	*									*			1855–1899
Holborn		*	*							*	*	*				1818–1889
Kensington																
Lambeth		*		*							*	*				1847–1899
Lewisham										*		*	*			1837–1899
City of London										*	*	*	*	*		1845–1902
East London															*	1865–1889
Poplar		*		*						*		*	*	*	*	1773–1900
Rotherhithe															*	
St George East															*	1836–1912
St George Martyr															*	1835–1914
St Martin-Fields																
St Olave															*	1848–1888
St Saviour										*			*		*	1829–1894
Stepney										*			*			1801–1856
Strand		*		*												1882–1892
Wandsworth & Clapham																
West London																
Whitechapel												*			*	1866–1900
Parishes*																
St Giles-Fields and St George, Bloomsbury										*		*	*		*	1836–1900
St George, Hanover Sq														*		1889–1897
St James-St John Clerkenwell																
St James, Westminster																
St Leonard, Shoreditch																
St Luke, Middlesex																
St Mary, Islington																
St Margaret-St John Westminster					*				*	*			*		*	1711–1853
St Mary, Newington																
St Marylebone		*	*	*						*	*	*		*	*	1769–1900
St Pancras Soperlane		*	*	*						*	*		*	*	*	1834–1931
St Sepulchre																

*Established with independent poor-law powers by Act of Parliament

[1]Includes infirmaries, hospitals, soldiers homes

WARDS	Account Books	Beadle's Books	Freeman Occupiers	Householders	Inhabitants	Non-Freemen	Orphans	Poll Tax	Precinct Minutes	Voters Lists	Wardmote Inquest	Dates
Aldersgate, w. and w.			*					*	*			1678-1849
Aldgate			*	*				*		*		1678-1882
Bassieshaw			*	*	*			*				1678-1849
Billingsgate								*		*		1678-1839
Bishopsgate, w. and w.								*				1678-1694
Blackfriars*							*	*				1689-1789
Bread-Street			*		*			*				1678-1849
Bridge				*				*	*		*	1627-1827
Broad-Street			*					*				1678-1849
Candlewick								*			*	1678-1862
Castle Baynard								*				1678-1693
Cheap			*					*				1678-1851
Coleman-Street			*					*				1678-1850
Cordwainer		*	*		*			*				1678-1850
Cornhill					*			*				1678-1853
Cripplegate, w. and w.												-----
Dowgate							*	*				1678-1698
Farringdon, within			*					*				1678-1843
Farringdon, without			*					*				1666-1850
Langbourn								*				1692-1823
Lime-Street			*					*	*	*		1678-1892
Portsoken								*				1678-1698
Queenhithe								*				1678-1695
Tower				*				*				1678-1817
Vintry				*	*			*				1678-1827
Walbrook	*		*		*			*				1678-1850

Westminster--

1. Peter Street
2. Mill Bank or Horse-Ferry
3. Sanctuary and Deanery
4. Upper King-Street
5. Lower King-Street
6. New Palace-Yard
7. Long-Ditch
8. Petty France
9. Tuthill-Street

These records are cataloged under England, London, London: Civil Jurisdiction, Election, Guardian and Ward, and Taxation. There are few cross references.

*Not given as a ward in the Parliamentary Gazeteer, 1840.

LEGAL RECORDS: County

	Dates Covered	No. of Rolls
DEEDS AND OTHER LEGAL INSTRUMENTS		
Indexes		
Middlesex		
Alphabetical Indices to the Middlesex County Deed Registers. Indexed.		22

CHURCH RECORDS: Church of England

	Dates Covered	No. of Rolls
MARRIAGE RECORDS		
Papers		
Canterbury Province		
Faculty Office		
Marriage Allegations	1632–1851	203
Registry of the Vicar–General		
Marriage Allegations	1660–1851	250
Carlisle		
Marriage License Bonds, Indexed	1668–1824	6
Durham		
Marriage Bonds		
Durham	1594–1782	1
Northumberland	1664–1672	
Exeter		
Marriage Licenses, Indexed	1523–1762	6
Devon		
Marriage Licenses, Indexed	1736–1837	4
Gloucester		
Marriage Allegations	1637–1823	33
Lichfield and Coventry		
Marriage Licenses, Bonds and Affidavits	1636–1880	458
Whittington, Staffs.		
Marriage Licenses, Bonds	1672–1852	1
Penkridge, Staffs.		
Marriage Licenses, Bonds	1709–1852	2
Packwood, Warws.		
Marriage Licenses, Bonds	1711–1855	1
Lincoln		
Marriage Bonds	1837–1885	2

	Dates Covered	No. of Rolls
Indexes		
<u>London Diocese</u>		
Index of Marriage License Allegations. Index Library, British Record Society, vols. 62-66.	1597-1859	
Chelmsford		
Index of Marriage Licenses	1665-1853	1
City of London		
Index to Marriage Registers of St. Michael Paternoster Royal and St. Martin Vintry.	1558-1837	1
Southwark		
Alphabetical Index to Marriage Licenses.	1700-1900	6
PROBATE RECORDS		
Papers		
<u>London Diocese</u>		
Archdeaconry		
Colchester	1495-1858	43
Essex	1400-1857	40
London	1368-1807	200
Middlesex	1538-1857	87
Commissary Court		
Essex, Hertfordshire, Middlesex	1368-1857	303
London	1449-1857	587
Consistory Court	1362-1857	49
Court of the Arches, Canterbury	1614-1821	68
Court of Delegates	1662-1837	2
Peculiars		
Deanery of the Arches (cataloged under Kent, Shortham, Croydon)	1665-1816	23
Deanery of Bocking	1627-1857	7
Dean and Chapter of Westminster	1504-1829	39

	Dates Covered	No. of Rolls
Good Easter	1618-1847	2
Liberty Sokens	1659-1753	1
St. Katherine by the Tower	1689-1818	3
Writtle with Roxwell	1618-1851	3
Prerogative Court of Canterbury	1611-1837	1

Indexes

London Diocese

Peculiars

Bocking, Good Easter and Writtle
    Calendar of Wills   1617-1691   5

Dean and Chapter of Westminster
    Calendar of Wills and Administrations   1504-1858   3
    Calendar of Wills   1698-1803   1

CHURCH RECORDS: Nonconformist

	Dates Covered	No. of Rolls
GENERAL RECORDS		
Papers		
Fleet Prison		
Clandestine Baptisms and Marriages, Fleet Prison Chapel, London; Mayfair Chapel, Westminster; Kings Bench Prison Chapel and the Mint, Southwark. Indexed.	1667–1754	91
Dr. Williams' Library		
Non-parochial Certificates of Births in London	1800–1834	1
Non-parochial Registers of Births	1815–1824	5
Presbyterian, Independent, and Baptist Certificates of Birth, London and Elsewhere. Indexed.	1762–1837	110
DENOMINATIONAL RECORDS		
Baptist		
City of London		
White's Alley		
Minutes and Proceedings	1681–1761	3
Calvinist		
City of London		
Swiss Calvinist Church		
Registration of Those Attending Catechism Instruction.	1762–1801	1 it.
French Protestant		
City of London		
St. Martin Orgar		
Birth Briefs and Pew Assignments	1691–1763	2
Receipts and Accounts Payable	1691–1763	1
Register of Parishioners	1760–1764	1

	Dates Covered	No. of Rolls
Independent		
City of London		
Church of Christ		
Minute Book	1806–1809	1 it.
Lime Street Independent		
Minute Book	1728–1764	1
Nightingale Lane, Church of Christ		
Minute Book, List of Members	1715–1762	2 it.
Lutheran, Hamburg		
City of London		
Holy Trinity the Less		
Kirchen Buch. Communicants, accounts, lists of school children, confirmations.	1669–1849	1
Methodist		
City of London		
Wesleyan Methodist Metropolitan Registry, Paternoster Row		
Parchment Certificates of Births, Baptisms	1818–1841	
Certificates #10276–91 are Baptisms at English Chapel, Stockholm, Sweden.	1838	25
Presbyterian		
Camden/Holborn		
National Scots Chapel, St. Pancras, Regents Square		
Pew Books	1827–1932	1
Islington		
Highbury Park Chapel		
Roll of Communicants	1854–1940	1
Scots Chapel, Canonbury		
Roll of Communicants	1879–1935	1 it.
Trinity Chapel, Canonbury		
Roll of Members and Communicants	1879–1928	1
City of London		
Scots Church, Founders Hall, Lothbury		
Sessions Book	1717–1771	1
Scots Presbytery		
Minute Books	1772–1899	7

	Dates Covered	No. of Rolls
London North		
Minutes of Presbytery	1888–1892	2 it.
London Wall		
Admissions and Disjunctions	1796–1843	2 it.
Southwark		
Hamilton Chapel, Camberwell		
Roll of Communicants	1867–1935	2 it.
Camberwell Chapel		
Roll of Communicants	1869–1880	1 it.
Westminster		
Presbyterian Chapel		
Session Book, Cash Books, and Minute Books	1786–1859	1
Scots Chapel, Swallow Street		
Session Minutes and Cash Books	1770–1846	1

Reformed

City of London

Austin Friars, Dutch Reformed Church		
Attestations, Confessions of Guilt	1570–1872	13
Membership Registers	1550–1873	
Consistory Members, Student Fund	1576–1685	13
Written in Dutch		
St. James French Royal Chapel		
Marriage Licenses	1700–1754	1

Roman Catholic

Bermondsey		
Register of Children	1877–1894	1
Southwark		
Register of Children	1878–1895	1

Society of Friends

City of London

London Yearly Meeting		
Advices	1675–1756	1 it.

	Dates Covered	No. of Rolls
Indexes		
Jewish		
Bevis Marks Congregation Index to Synagogue Records	1689-1909	1
Methodist		
Wesleyan Methodist Metropolitan Registry Index to Parchment Certificates of Births and Baptisms. Arranged alphabetically.	1818-1841	1

CORPORATE RECORDS

	Dates Covered	No. of Rolls
Papers		
British Lying-In Hospital		
List of Children Born and Baptized	1788-1814	1
Chelsea Hospital		
Military Records of Irish Casuals	1836	
Special Constables	1831,1846	
Accounts of Families of Servicemen Receiving Payment and Subsidies	1796-1800	1
East India Company, Poplar Borough (additional records of the East are noted in Section IV)		
Almshouse Accounts	1709-1810	1 it.
Burials	1825-1855	1 it.
Journal and Records of Almshouses	1808-1849	1 it.
Minute Book	1655-1659	1
Pension Receipt Book	1813-1865	1 it.
New Zealand Company		
Embarkation Register	1839-1850	1
Emigration Register	1839-1850	1
Royal Academy of Arts		
Register of Students	1769-1922	1
Trinity House[3]		
Apprenticeship Indensures	1780, 1818-1845	1
Civil Records	1780-1880	7
Petitions	19th C.	57

---

[3]Indexed in Genealogists Magazine, Vol. 16, #8. Trinity House is an almshouse for retired merchant navy captains who are over 60 years of age, disabled and/or without property or other income, and not connected to any parish or charitable institution.

GUILDS[1]	Accounts	Apprentices	Court and Livery	Freemen	Cemetery Inscriptions	Minute Books	Oath Rolls	Orphans	Wardens	Dates
Armourers		*		*						1416-1663
Brewers		*	*	*						1685-1824
Carpenters		*	*	*						1654-1892
Coachmakers and Coach Harness Makers		*								1677-1800
Curriers		*								1628-1840
Drapers*		*								1615-1750
Fishmongers*		*		*						1537-1650
Fruiterers		*	*	*						1749-1903
Glovers		*	*	*						1680-1851
Grocers*									*	1345-1907
Ironmongers*			*							17 July 1924
Mercers*					*					1600-1900
Painters and Paint-stainers		*		*						1658-1950
Pattenmakers		*	*	*						1673-1900
Paviours	*	*	*	*			*			1565-1853
Pewterers				*						n.d.
Plumbers			*	*						1696-1794
Shipwrights		*		*						1694-1900
Stationers										1562-1900
Tacklehouse and Ticketporters	*					*	*			1600-1900
Turners		*	*	*						1604-1872
Wax Chandlers		*		*				*		1596-1857
White Bakers		*	*	*						1565-1935
The Livery**			*				*			1696-1836

(All dates are inclusive. Some years
are missing in most categories)

[1]The Guilds are filed in the Card Catalog under England, London, London, Occupations, and then in strict alphabetical order according to the title of the record. This requires reading every card to locate multiple entries for each company. For example, Stationers' Records appear under Stationers Company and the Worshipful Company of Stationers.

*Among the Twelve Great Companies. In 1840, there were 89 companies in London.

**The Livery was the voting or preferred body of members in each company.

<u>PERSONAL RECORDS</u>

	Dates Covered	No. of Rolls
MANUSCRIPT COLLECTIONS		
Bernau, Charles Allan		
Correspondence and Genealogical Research. 1st Series.		19
Circular of the Genealogical Cooperative Search Club, organized in London in 1913. (Genealogical Society of Utah), 1 vol. manuscript.		
Culleton Genealogical Agency		
Research Notes on English Families.		41
Genealogical Manuscripts in the British Museau. Arranged alphabetically.		6
Index to Names of Persons Found in Unidentified Genealogical Collections. Various counties of England. Indexed. (Genealogical Society of Utah)		1
Gwyn, Henry		
Historical Notices of St. Bartholomew by the Exchange. Includes parish register transcripts, monumental inscriptions, church notes, rectors, benefactors, miscellaneous notes, and pedigrees. (Guildhall Library)	1558-1711	2 it.
PEDIGREES		
Boyd, Sir Percival		
Pedigrees of London Citizens. Abstracted at random from London guild records with parish registers and wills added. (Genealogical Society of Utah)	c.1600-1800	135
Pedigrees from London Visitations	1568-1687	1 it.
Phillimore, W.P.W.		
County Pedigrees for London and Nottingham. (Genealogical Society of Utah)		1 it.

	Dates Covered	No. of Rolls

MONUMENTAL INSCRIPTIONS

Bloom, James Harvey

    Monumental Inscriptions from Old Churchyard
      next to St. Paul's Church, Clapham, Lambeth;
      Mounted Newspaper Clippings of Deaths, 1 vol.
      manuscript.   c.1900

Snell, Frederick Simon

    Index to Monumental Inscriptions of Hampstead
      Parish Church and Churchyard to 1888, 1 vol.
      manuscript. (Genealogical Society of Utah)   1888

RESEARCH AIDS

	Dates Covered	No. of Rolls
GOVERNMENT RECORDS: City		
City of London		
Citizen's List. Copied by Sir Percival Boyd, 1 vol. manuscript.	1651	
Divided Houses in the City of London, 1637: A Census of Multiple Dwellings in and around London. Copied by T. C. Dale. Indexed, 1 vol. manuscript.	1637	
List of Members of the Common Council. Indexed.	1780-1879	1 it.
GOVERNMENT RECORDS: Local		
Vital Records		
Directory of Parishes and Dates in Pallott's Marriage Index for London and Middlesex, 1 vol. manuscript.	1780-1837	
Directory to the Registers and Microfilms of Clandestine Baptisms and Marriages in Fleet Prison Chapel, London; Mayfair Chapel, Westminster; Kings Bench Prison Chapel and the Mint, Southwark.	1667-1754	1 it.
Vital Records of Poplar Chapel. Compiled by John Southerdon Burn. Indexed, 1 vol. manuscript.	1584-1799	
Burial Grounds		
Burials for St. Benet Fink, 1538-1845 and St. Peter le Poor, 1561-1853. Compiled by Sir Percival Boyd. Male names only, 1 vol. manuscript.	1538-1845 1561-1853	
Index to Burials in the London Area. Compiled by Sir Percival Boyd. Male names only, 16 vols. manuscripts.	1538-1835	
LEGAL RECORDS		
City of London		
Key List to Old Bailey Sessions Records. Includes session rolls, entry books, recognizances and estreats.	1727-1835	1 it.

	Dates Covered	No. of Rolls
CHURCH RECORDS		
Marriage Records		
Index to Marriage Licenses, Chelmsford. Compiled by Robert Hollingworth Browne.	1665-1853	1
Probate Records		
Index to Register of Wills and Administrations, Episcopal Consistory Court, Bishop of London. Compiled by James Harvey Bloom.	1313-1548	1 it.
CORPORATE RECORDS		
Guilds		
Members of London Guilds. Abstracted at random from apprenticeship and other records by Sir Percival Boyd, 4 vols. manuscripts.		
St. Peters College, Westminster		
A List of Scholars of St. Peters College, Westminster, as They Were Elected to Christ Church College, Oxford, and Trinity College, Cambridge, 1561-1788; with additions to 1818. Compiled by Joseph Welch.	1561-1788	1 it.
The Times, London		
Index to Births, Marriages and Deaths in the London Times. Includes a 5-page How to Use Announcements Appearing in the London Times.	1785-1933	99
PERSONAL RECORDS		
Individuals		
Nonconformists of London. Extracts of specific surnames from 193 chapels made by Ira William Mount.		2
Monumental Inscriptions		
An Obituary; being an Index of the Monuments and Burials Records in Lyson's Environs of London, with a few additions from other sources. Compiled by Major John Beach Whitmore.		2 it.

	Dates Covered	No. of Rolls

RESEARCH AIDS

Genealogical Society of Utah Guides

    County Keys. Reference volumes for genealogical
    research in London. (These volumes are updated
    frequently and used as a tool by reference con-
    sultants in the British Section of the Library.
    They are not on the reference table.) 4 vols.
    manuscript

    Parishes of London. Compiled by David E. Gardner,
    1 vol. manuscript.

    Pre-1858 English Probate Jurisdictions: Probate
    Courts in London. Compiled by the Research
    Department of the Genealogical Society, 1 vol.
    manuscript.

    Records of the Chancery Court, London and Judicial
    Chancery Proceedings, Equity Side. Register of
    contents. With an introduction on the use of court
    records by David E. Gardner, 1 vol. manuscript.   1386–1875